THE STORY OF JUDITH

IN GERMAN AND ENGLISH LITERATURE

BY

EDNA PURDIE

(LECTURER IN GERMAN, UNIVERSITY COLLEGE OF NORTH WALES, BANGOR)

(Thesis approved for the Degree of Doctor of Literature
in the University of London)

PARIS

LIBRAIRIE ANCIENNE HONORÉ CHAMPION

5, QUAI MALAQUAIS. VIᵉ

— 1927 —

THE STORY OF JUDITH
IN GERMAN AND ENGLISH LITERATURE

THE STORY OF JUDITH

IN GERMAN AND ENGLISH LITERATURE

BY

EDNA PURDIE

(LECTURER IN GERMAN, UNIVERSITY COLLEGE OF NORTH WALES, BANGOR)

———

(Thesis approved for the Degree of Doctor of Literature
in the University of London)

PARIS
LIBRAIRIE ANCIENNE HONORÉ CHAMPION
5, QUAI MALAQUAIS, VIᵉ
— 1927 —

PREFATORY NOTE

It would be impossible for me to publish this short study of the tale of Judith as reflected in the two literatures of Germany and England without an expression of deep gratitude to Professor Robert Priebsch (University College, London), to whose help and inspiration the work, both in its inception and during its completion, owes more than can be estimated.

My thanks are also due to Professor J. G. Robertson (University of London) for much kind advice and encouragement, to Dr. Rudolf Hittmair (Innsbruck) for very kind bibliographical assistance, particularly in the part of the work dealing with modern German literature from 1914 to 1921, to Professor H. G. Fiedler (Oxford) for kindly drawing my attention to the versions on p. 22. (list of addenda) and to the Director of the Stadtbibliothek, Aachen (Dr. M. Müller) for his courtesy in transcribing the "programme" of *Judith* (1763) which constitutes Appendix B. For other passages transcribed I am indebted to Dr. W. E. Delp (Royal Holloway College), to Dr. N. Busch (Stadtbibliothek, Riga), and to the Director of the Gymnasium Josephinum, Hildesheim ; while to the courtesy of the authorities of the Universitätsbibliothek, Leipzig, the Klosterbibliothek, Engelberg, the Bürgerbibliothek, Luzern, and the Staatsbibliothek, München, I owe the opportunity of examining the MSS. of plays in their possession. To them, as well as to the authorities of the National Library, Berlin, the University Library, Innsbruck, the Museum Ferdinandum, Innsbruck, and the Public Libraries at Graz, Hildesheim and Salzburg, I offer my acknowledgments. I need hardly add that the work could not have been done without the wonderful resources of the British Museum.

Finally, I am greatly indebted to the donor and trustees of the Tiarks Fund for assistance in the publication of the work.

EDNA PURDIE.

Bangor. N. Wales. 1926.

I

CHRONOLOGICAL AND BIBLIOGRAPHICAL SURVEY OF THE VERSIONS OF THE JUDITH STORY IN GERMAN AND ENGLISH LITERATURE

(Including some records of and evidence for versions not extant)

1. (9th century) *Versus de Judit et Holofernem.*

    A few strophes (tercets of trochaic catalectic. tetrameters) of a Latin poem, giving beginning and end of the narrative. Reprinted in E. Du Méril : *Poésies populaires antérieures au 12ᵐᵉ siècle*, Paris, 1843. pp. 184-185 ; and with six additional strophes from a 3rd (Brussels) MS. in E. Dümmler : *Rhythmen aus der Karolingischen Zeit*, Zeitschrift für deutsches Altertum, vol. XXIII, p. 266. Berlin, 1879.

    (These verses, although in Latin, have been included as probably contributing to the knowledge of the story in Germany).

2. (10th century ?) *Judith.* MS. Cotton Vitellius A XV. British Museum.

    Fragment (the last three cantos) of an Old English poem in alliterative verse, probably belonging to the 2nd decade of the 10th century.

    v. A. S. Cook : *Judith : an Old English Epic Fragment.* Boston, 1889 (2nd ed.)

    and T. Gregory Foster : *Judith*, in *Quellen und Forschungen zur Sprach = und Culturgeschichte der germanischen Völker*, vol. LXXI. Strassburg, 1892.

3. (10th century ?). Aelfric : *Homily on the Book of Judith.*

    Two fragmentary MSS. of this rhythmical version of the Book of Judith are to be found in codices (of the 12th century) containing other works of Aelfric :

    Corpus Christi Coll : 303 (fol. 356-362).

    Cotton Otho B X (fol. 29a-30b).

    v. B. Assmann in *Anglia* vol. X. pp. 76 ff.

4. (11th century ?) *Judith.* in Vorauer HS. (12th century).

    An early Middle High German narrative poem (called the " ältere Judith ") probably dating from the 11th century and belonging to the " Spielmann " poetry.

    An exact reprint in J. Diemer : *Deutsche Gedichte des XI. u. XII. Jahrhunderts.* Wien, 1849. pp. 117-123.

v. also A. Waag : *Kleinere Deutsche Gedichte des XI. und XII. Jahrhunderts.* Halle, 1890, pp. 36-41.

E. Sievers : " Zur älteren Judith " in *Rhythmisch-melodische Studien.* Heidelberg, 1912, pp. 112 ff.

A. Wallner : *Pfaffendichtung* in *Beiträge zur Geschichte der deutschen Sprache und Literatur* (Paul u. Braune) vol. XLIII, pp. 181 ff.

Valentin Teuber : *Die mittelalterlichen Gedichte von der Judith in ihrem Verhältnisse zu einander untersucht.* Programm des Kommunalobergymnasiums in Komotau. Komotau, 1906/1907.

and G. Ehrismann . *Geschichte der deutschen Literatur bis zum Ausgang des Mittelalters.* Teil II. 1. (Frühmittelhochdeutsche Zeit). München, 1922, pp. 103-108.

5. (11th-12th century). *Judith.* Vorauer HS.

A long didactic poem (called the „ jüngere Judith ") in the same MS. as No. 4.

Reprint in Diemer : *op. cit.,* pp. 127-180.

v. J. Pirig : *Untersuchungen über die sogenannte jüngere Judith.* Bonn, 1881. (Pirig points out the resemblances in this poem to the *Itala* version of the Apocryphal book).

v. also G. Ehrismann : *op. cit.,* pp. 108-110.

6. 13th Century. *Judith.* A poem of the „ Teutonic Order ", preserved in one MS. of the late 14th or early 15th century —part of a parchment codex found in the Königliche Bibliothek, Stuttgart, and shewn by inscriptions to have belonged to the library of the Teutonic Order at Mergentheim.

v. *Zeitschrift für deutsche Philologie* vol. XXXIII, p. 430, Halle, 1901. (A. Schaer : Philologischer Verein, Strassburg, 1901). A full description of the MS. in C. H. G. Helm : *Das Buch der Makkabäer.* Bibliothek des Literarischen Vereins Stuttgard. Vol. CCXXXIII (p. VII). Tübingen, 1904.

v. also Karl Helm : *Zum md. Gedicht von der Judith* in Paul und Braune *Beiträge,* vol. XLIII, pp. 163-8, and in *Anz. f. d. A.,* vol. LXII, p. 149. A discussion of the poem in Max Hering : *Judith, ein mitteldeutsches Gedicht des 13. Jahrhunderts.* Halle, 1907.

v. also *Judith. Ein mitteldeutsches Gedicht aus dem 13. Jahrhundert.* Aus der Stuttgarter HS. zum ersten Male herausgegeben v. R. Palgen, Halle, 1924.

7. 13th Century (ca. 1250). The narrative of *Judith* in Heinrich von München's continuation of the *Weltchronik* of Rudolf von Ems, taken direct from the Vulgate account.

v. Gœdeke : *Grundriss der Geschichte der deutschen Dichtung* (2te Auflage) Bd. I (Dresden, 1884) p. 126.

A. F. C. Vilmar : *Die zwei Rezensionen und die Hand-schriftenfamilie der Weltchronik Rudolfs von Ems.* Marburg, 1839. and Rudolf von Ems : *Weltchronik.* in *Deutsche Texte des Mittelalters* vol. XX. ed. G. Ehrismann. Berlin, 1915. For an additional fragment (discovered in 1862) dealing with Judith and Holofernes, v. A. Edzardi and E. Mogk : " Kopenhagener Bruchstücke von Rudolfs Welt-chronik " in *Germania* vol. XXVII, pp. 68 ff. Wien, 1882.

8. (13th-14th century). Heinrich von Meissen (Frauenlob) *Judith.* Sprüche III. (Frauen b. 417) in *Heinrichs von Meissen des Frauenlobes Leiche, Sprüche, Streitgedichte und Lieder.* ed. L. Ettmüller. Quedlinburg und Leipzig, 1843. (pp. 232-3).

    A Short " Spruch " giving the story of Judith as an example of Nemesis and the fall of man from high estate. cp. Chaucer : Monkes Tale (De Oloferno) in *Canterbury Tales (Text)* in *Complete Works* ed. W. W. Skeat, Oxford, 1894. (pp. 261-2 and 243), where the narrative illustrates a similar idea.

9. 1536. Joachim Greff : *Tragoedia des Buchs Judith.* Wittemberg, 1536. Academic drama. (Copy in British Museum).

    v. Goedeke : *Grundriss der Geschichte der deutschen Dicht-ung* (2te Aufl.) Bd. II (Dresden 1886) p. 357.
    Gottsched : *Nöthiger Vorrath zur Geschichte der deutschen dramatischen Dichtkunst.* Leipzig 1757-65, vol. I, p. 75. and *Intermédiaire des Chercheurs et Curieux*, XIVe année. Paris, 1881, 10 Oct. col. 638.

10. 1536 (?) Sixt Birck : *Judith.* Latin drama. (Copy in British Museum).

    v. J. Bolte : Introduction to Birck's *Susanna*, in *Latein-ische Literaturdenkmäler des XV. und XVI. Jahrhunderts* No. 8. Berlin, 1893. (pp. v and vii.).

11. 1539. Sixt Birck, or Xystus Betuleius : *Judith*, eine schön[1] History in Spylsweiss für die Augen gestelt, wie man in Kriegesläuffen, besonders so man von wegen der Ehr Gottes angefochten würt, um hülff zu Gott dem Herrn flehend ruffen soll. Augsburg, 1539, and Strassburg, 1559.
    German version of the story, apparently written before No. 10.
    v. J. Nysaeus, Xysti Betuleii Vita, in *Lactantii Opera*, ed. Xystus Betuleius, Basileae, 1563. b. 4. (Copy in British Museum).
    v. Goedeke : *Grundriss* ed. cit. Bd. II, p. 345.

---

   1. For convenience of printing it has been found desirable to adopt the modern designation of « Umlaut » throughout.

and Gottsched : *Nöthiger Vorrath zur Geschichte der deutschen dramatischen Dichtkunst.* Leipzig, 1757-65. II. Theil. p. 218.

12. 1542. Wolfgang Schmeltzl : *Judith.* Wien, 1542.

An Austrian academic drama.

v. Goedeke : *Grundriss* ed. cit. Bd. II, p. 404.

Serapeum, Jahrgang XXV (Nr. 18) Leipzig, 30. Sept. 1864. p. 275.

E. Devrient : *Geschichte der deutschen Schauspielkunst.* Leipzig 1848. vol. I. p. 128.

A. Mayer : *Wiens Buchdruckergeschichte 1482-1882.* Wien, 1883-7, vol. I, p. 48.

F. Spengler : *Wolfgang Schmeltzl* in *Beiträge zur Ge--schichte der deutschen Literatur und des geistigen Lebens in Österreich.* Heft III. Wien, 1883.

The original text of this work is one of the libri desiderati. In 1821 a copy was in the possession of J. F. Castelli.

v. J. F. C. *Dramatische Seltenheiten* in *Zeitung für die elegante Welt,* Nr. 120-121, Leipzig, 1821. This seems to be the volume recorded as having passed into the University Library at Graz, but which has since been lost. A MS. copy, made by Karl Weinhold in 1854, was seen by Spengler before writing the above-mentioned monograph. (Spengler *op. cit.* p. 40.)

(There is no copy in the Nationalbibliothek at Vienna).

13. (Before 1548). Ralph Radcliff : *De Judith Fortitudine.*

A lost academic drama, mentioned in Bishop Bale's *Scriptorum illustrium majoris Britanniae catalogus.* Basileae, 1557-9, i, 700.

v. E. K. Chambers : *The Mediaeval Stage.* Oxford, 1903. vol. II, p. 197 and p. 218.

and James de Rothschild : *Le Mistère du Viel Testament.* Paris, 1878-91. Vol. V, p. cxliv.

14. 1551. Hans Sachs : *Judith.* Ein Comedi mit 16 personen zu recidirn und hat fünff actus.

v. Hans Sachs : *Werke* ed. A. von Keller. 10 vols. Tübingen, 1870-76. (Bibliothek des Literarischen Vereins Stuttgart, CII-CVI, CX, CXV, CXXI, CXXV, CXXXI-CXXXII). vol. VI, pp. 56 ff.

15. 1554. Hans Sachs : *Die Judit mit Holoferne ob der belegerung der Stat Bethulia.* Nürnberg, 1554.

A short narrative poem.

v. Hans Sachs : *Werke* ed. cit. vol. I, p. 246.

cp. also Hans Sachs : *Der ehrenspiegel der zwölf durch-lauchtigen frawen dess alten Testaments. Werke* ed. cit. vol. I, p. 207.

16. 1555. *Historia Judith.* Acted at Hildesheim (Andreanum).

v. Goedeke : *Grundriss* ed. cit. Bd. II, p. 398.

Rothschild : *op. cit.* vol. V, p. CXLVIII.

Reinhard Müller : *Beiträge zur Geschichte des Schul-theaters am Gymnasium Josephinum in Hildesheim.* Progr. Hildesheim, 1901, p. 5.

and K. Th. Gaedertz : *Archivalische Nachrichten über die Theaterzustände von Hildesheim, Lübeck, Lüneburg im 16. und 17. Jahrhundert.* Bremen, 1888, p. 3.

('Im lütken Fastelabend spielte der Schulmeister v. S. Andreas (Rector) Lorenz Müller utte dem olden Testamente *Judith*, ging fein zu. Der Rath schenkede ihm 10 fl. und hatten lassen ein Palatium auf dem Markede bawen, kostete auch viel.'

Ex Schnarmacheri annalibus. Museum, Hildesheim.)

There is no copy, or periocha, of this play in any library in Hildesheim. [1]

17. 1556. *Holophernes.* Lost drama, known to have been performed in 1566 at Hatfield House by order of Sir Thomas Pope to entertain the Princess Elizabeth.

v. Chronicle MS. Cotton Vitell : F 5. British Museum (containing journal of events about London from 4 Edward VI to 5 Elizabeth, *i. e.* 1563).

and Thos. Warton : *Life of Sir Thomas Pope.* London, 1780, p. 87.

18. 1564. Ein schön Biblisch Spyl, beide lehrhaft und lustig, *Judith* genent. Newlich zu Strassburg durch ein junge Burgerschafft zu gemeiner besserung offentlich gespilet im iar 1564. Getruckt zu Strassburg bey Thiebolt Berger. (Copy of this play in the Stadtbibliothek, Weimar. A woodcut of Holofernes' tent outside Bethulia adorns the title-page, and at the bottom of the latter is written in ink : cum : Balthasari Cordi Smalkaldani con[s]tat (?) (following single letter and one word indecipherable.)

There is no clue to the authorship of the play [2].

v. Goedeke : *Grundriss* ed. cit. Bd. II, p. 390.

and Rothschild : *op. cit.* vol. V, p. CXLVIIJ.

---

1. This remark is based on information kindly supplied by the authorities of the Stadtbücherei, Hildesheim.

2. These particulars, together with a synopsis of the contents of the drama (which is in seven acts, with a Prologue and " Beschluss ", and requires a large number of actors) were kindly sent me by Miss W. E. Delp, who examined the copy in Weimar.

19. 1565. *Judith und Holofernes*. " Volksschauspiel " performed at Vomperfeld, Tirol.

> v. Adalbert Sikora': *Zur Geschichte der Volksschauspiele in Tirol*. p. 9. (Separatabdruck aus dem *Archiv für Theatergeschichte*, herausgeg. H. Devrient, vol. II, pp. 1-55.)
>
> These Volksschauspiele appear to have been closely connected with the Jesuit drama. v. *ibid* : p. 11 and A. Sikora : *Zur Geschichte der Volksschauspiele in Tirol* in *Zeitschrift des Ferdinandeums für Tirol und Vorarlberg*. 3. Folge. 50. Heft. Innsbruck, 1906, p. 369.

20. 1565. The famous history of the vertuous and Godly woman *Judyth*, wherein is declared the great myght of God : delivering his people out of the handes of theyr enemies, at what time soever they wyll truste in hys mercy and unfaynedly call upon his holye name.

> Translated into Englysh meter by Edward Jeninges, with a Preface or Exhortacyon to the same. Imprinted at London by Thomas Colwell. A. D. 1565. May 10. 8⁰.
>
> Title quoted by Hazlitt : *Collections and Notes*, 1867-76. London, 1876, p. 243, with the note : " This is one of the *libri desiderati*. I find it mentioned by most bibliographers ; but I never saw a copy, or heard of anyone who had ".

21. 1566. Ein spil von der *Belegerung der Statt Bethania* und wie sie Gott wunderlich durch ain wittfraw Judith genannt, die Holofernem den oberstē Hauptman im Läger umbracht, erlöset hat, nutzlich und lustig zu lesen, in Reym bescriben durch Samuelem Hebelum Cervimontanem. Gedruckt zu Wienn in Osterreich bey Caspar Stainhofer in St. Annenhof anno 1566.

> v. Goedeke : *Grundriss* ed. cit. Bd. II, p. 406.
> A. Mayer : *Wiens Buchdruckergeschichte* ed cit. vol. I, p. 102.
> Rothschild : *op. cit.* vol. V, p. CXLIX.
> and H. M. Schletterer : *Das deutsche Singspiel*. Augsburg, 1863, p. 169. (where the title is quoted with the name *Bethulia*, and the influence of the Reformation in the chorus tune " Eine feste Burg ist unser Gott " is noted).
> The drama has a dedication to the Council of Iglau.

22. 1566-67. *Judith and Holyfernes*. Lost ballad, printed by William Pekerynge in 1566-67, and entered in the Stationers' Register.

> v. E. Arber : *Transcript of the Registers of the Company of Stationers of London 1554-1640*. vol. I, Register A 154, b. London, 1875.

23. 1584. *Historie of Judith in the forme of a poeme* : penned in French by the noble poet G. Saluste, Lord of Bartas : Englished by Thomas Hudson. Edinburgh, 1584.

> Re-issued in London in 1608, with the later editions of Sylvester's Du Bartas, and reprinted in 1611 and 1613.
>
> v. *Dictionary of National Biography*, vol. XXVIII, p. 153.

24. 1588. (A) ballade intytuled the moste famous historye of *Judith and* (*H*)*olofernes.*

> Licensed, with two other didactic ballads (under the patronage of the Bishop of London) to Sampson Clerk in March 1588.   Lost ballad.
>
> v. E. Arber : *Transcript of the Registers of the Company of Stationers* ed. cit. vol. II, Register B. 227.
>
> and Hazlitt : *Bibliographical Collections and Notes on Early English Literature.* (2nd series, 1474-1700) London, 1882. p. 322.

25. 1591. Michael Drayton : *Harmonie of the Church.*

> Contains a version of the " praier of Judith " and the " song of Judith ".
>
> v. *The Harmony of the Church* by Michael Drayton. Now first reprinted from the edition of 1591. ed. A. Dyce. London, 1843. (Publications of the Percy Society, vol. VII) pp. 48-53.

26. 1592. Cornelius Schonaeus, or " Terentius Christianus " : *Judithae Constantia*, Haarlem, 1592.

> Latin scholastic drama " ad usum scholarum ".
>
> v. Goedeke : *Grundriss* ed. cit. Bd. II, p. 143.
>
> Rothschild : *op. cit.* vol. V, p. cxxj.
>
> and O. Francke : *Terenz und die lateinische Schulko-mödie in Deutschland.* Welmar, 1877. pp. 71 ff.
>
> A volume containing *Tobaeus, Juditha* and *Pseudostrat-iotes* was printed in London in 1595. A fragment of a translation of *Juditha* is contained in MS. Peniarth 350 A (Hengwrt 508) in the National Library of Wales, Aberystwyth. The MS. probably belongs to the early 17th century ; the fragment (containing the title, names of dramatis personae, prologue and part of the first speech of Holofernes, in unrhymed verse, written as prose) ends at page 9 (which is partly torn off). It may have been a school exercise ; the Latin text appears (in an Italian hand) on the even pages, the English translation (in a national hand) on the odd. The translation shews an attempt to reproduce the versification of the original.
>
> For a transcription of the translation and a description

of the MS. v. Gwen Ann Jones : *A Play of Judith* in *Modern Language Notes* XXXII, 1. Baltimore. Jan. 1917.

27. 1597. Henry Lok : *Sundry Christian Passions contained in two hundred Sonnets.* London, 1597.—a collection of 200 Spiritual Sonnets—contains one (Part I, Sonnet LXXXIII) which allegorises the story of Judith.

28. 1601. *Historie von der Judith.* Acted by the pupils of the College of St. Catherine at St. Gallen in 1601.

> v. Rothschild : *op. cit.* vol. V, p. CXLIX.
>
> E. Weller : *Annalen der poetischen National-Literatur der Deutschen im XVI. u. XVII. Jahrhundert.* Freiburg i /Brg. 1862-4. vol. II, p. 293.
>
> and J. Baechtold : *Geschichte der deutschen Literatur in der Schweiz.* Frauenfeld, 1892 (Anmerkungen, p. 61).

29. 1604. *Judith.* Acted at Freiburg i /Brg. in the autumn of 1604. Rehearsals for this play were held in the courtyard of the Rathaus, and the cost of performance (15 gulden 11 kreuzer) was paid by the Council.

> v. E. Eckhardt : *Alte Schauspiele aus dem Breisgau* (Sonderdruck) Freiburg i /Brg. 1906, pp. 187-188.
> Heinrich Schreiber : *Das Theater zu Freiburg.* Freiburg i /Brg. 1837, p. 22.
> and E. J. Leichtlen : *Zur Geschichte des Freiburger Theaters* (Freiburg i /Brg. ?) 1827, p. 26.

30. 1607. *Ein schön Meysterlied von der Gottsförchtigen Frawen Judith, wie sie Holopherno das Haupt abschlug.* Im bewerten Thon Hans Sachsen. Leipzig, 1607.

> A short narrative poem consisting of four complicated stanzas with a moral epilogue. (Copy in British Museum.)

31. 1618. Martin Böhme : Tragicomoedia. *Ein schön Teutsch Spiel Vom Holoferne und der Judith.* The first of *Drei geistliche Comoedien*, Wittenberg, 1618.

> v. Goedeke : *Grundriss* ed. cit. Bd. II, p. 376.
> Rothschild : *op. cit.* vol. V, p. CXLIX.
> Gottsched (*Nöthiger Vorrath* ed. cit. I. Theil, p. 163) dates the comedies 1608. H. H. Borcherdt (*Andreas Tscherning. Ein Beitrag zur Literatur =* und Kulturgeschichte des XVII. Jahrhunderts. München u. Leipzig, 1912) suggests they may have been published in 1608 and reprinted in 1618. (Copy — very badly printed — in Preussische Staatsbibliothek, Berlin. Yq. 3201).

32. 1635. Martin Opitz : *Judith.* Breslau, 1635.

A " Singspiel " or opera text, derived from an Italian source.

v. *Martin Opitzen von Boberfeld* : *Teutsche Gedichte.* herausgeg. D. W. Triller, Frankfurt a /Main, 1746. vol. III, pp. 73-101 and (for a discussion of Opitz's relation to his Italian source) Anton Mayer : *Quelle und Entstehung von Opitzens Judith* in *Euphorion* XX, (1913) Leipzig u. Wien, 1913, pp. 39-53.

33. 1640. *Holofernes Assyriorum Dux.* Coram Paride Archiepiscopo. P. Aemilian Pirckel e S. Petro. 3. Dez. 1640. Salzburg (Benedictine Academy or University).

Programme (Latin and German) in the Öffentliche Studienbibliothek, Salzburg. (3956. I).

v. also H. F. Wagner : *Theaterwesen in Salzburg* in *Mitteilungen der Gesellschaft für Salzburger Landeskunde* XXXIII. (1893) Salzburg, 1893. pp. 260-1.

Pirckel (1605-1651) was Professor of Rhetoric in S. Lambrecht in Steiermark. v. Wagner : *op: cit.* p. 328.

34. 1642. *Tragoedia von Holoferne*... Dessen Geschicht zu lesen ist in dem Buech Judith sonderlich am 13. Cap. Gehalten inn dem Churfürstlichen und Academischen Gymnasio der Societet Jesu zu Ingolstatt, den 6. Oct. anno 1642. Gedruckt zu Ingolstatt bei Gregorio Haenlin. 4°. 8 Bl.

Programme of Jesuit " Schuldrama ".

v. *Intermédiaire des Chercheurs et Curieux*, XIVme année. Paris, 1881. 10 Oct., col. 637.

E. Weller in *Serapeum.* Jahrgang XXV (Nr. 21) Leipzig, 15 Nov. 1864, p. 334.

Rothschild : *op. cit.* vol. V, p. cxxj.

Backer-Sommervogel : *Bibliothèque de la Compagnie de Jésus* (Bibliographie) vol. IV, col. 592. (under Ingolstadt) Bruxelles, Paris, 1893.

35. ca. 1642. Nicolaus Avancinus : *Fiducia in Deum* sive *Bethulia Liberata.* Latin Jesuit drama performed at Vienna in 1642. (The note " 1643 exhibita " appended to the title is corrected to 1642 from the Litt. ann. Coll. Viennens. by P. Bernhard Duhr, vol. II, p. 687, note 3. v. infra. Cp. N. Avancinus : *Poesis dramatica.* Coloniae, 1675. Pt. II, p. 360 and ff.)

v. P. Bahlmann : *Jesuitendramen der niederrheinischen Ordensprovinz* in *Centralblatt für Bibliothekswesen*, Beiheft XV (in vol. VI) Leipzig, 1896-7, p. 5.

and B. Duhr, S. J. *Geschichte der Jesuiten in den Ländern deutscher Zunge* vol. II, Freiburg i /Brg. 1913, p. 687.

36. 1646. Andreas Tscherning : M. Opitzen *Judith*, auffs neu aussge-
fertigt ; worzu das vördere Theil der Historie sampt den Melo-
deyen auff iedwedes Chor beygefüget von Andreas Tscherning.
Rostock, 1646.

> An expansion of Opitz's " Singspiel " by the addition of
> two introductory acts, with the object of making it conform
> to the usual five-act play of the Jesuit " Schuldrama "
> type.
>
> v. H. H. Borcherdt : *Andreas Tscherning*. Ein Beitrag
> zur Literatur = und Kulturgeschichte des XVII. Jahr-
> hunderts. München u. Leipzig, 1912, ch. XI, pp. 107 ff.

37. 1647. *Tragoedia Mundi*, oder Lauff der jetzigen Wellt durch
Undergang König Arphaxats, Hochmuott Königs Nebucodo-
nosors Wütterey Holofernis und Starkhmüethigkeit der Helldin
Judith.   Acted at Luzern in 1647, May 1651, and sub-
sequently.   MS. in the Bürgerbibliothek, Luzern. (187
fol. 210 pp.)

> A favourite drama (requiring two days for represent-
> ation) of which Act II is concerned with Judith and Holo-
> fernes, while Act I deals with Arphaxat's fall, and Act
> III presents the symbolical triumph of Religion in the
> world over the forces of Evil. (cp. S. Matthew 21).
>
> v. Catalogue of MSS. Bürgerbibliothek, Luzern.
> Rothschild : *op. cit.* vol. V, p. CL.
> E. Weller : *Annalen* ed. cit. vol. II, p. 294.
> J. Baechtold : *Geschichte der deutschen Literatur in der
> Schweiz.* Frauenfeld, 1892, p. 466. Anm. pp. 151, 152.
> and *Der Geschichtsfreund.* Mittheilungen des histor-
> ischen Vereins der fünf Orte. vol. XVII. Einsiedeln, 1861.
> (P. G. Morel : *Das geistliche Drama, vom 12. bis 19. Jahr-
> hundert, in den fünf Orten und besonders in Einsiedeln* p. 85).

38. 1648. Christian Rose : *Holofern... allen des Teutsch=Landes
Friedens-Störern und Blut=gierigen Kriegern in einem lustigen
Schau-Spiel zur anderen Probe der Rhetorischen Mutter=Spraache
vorgestellet...* In welchem / (nebst vielen wol = mercklichen
Lehr = Puncten und Seufftzerlein / die in bedrangten Zeiten
zugebrauchen) auch etzlich=anmutige Concerten / von 3 Stim-
men / sampt einem Basso Continuô / sein mit = einverleibet / so
dem Wercke gleichsam eine Seele geben ! Hamburg, 1648.

> v. Heinrich Begemann : *M. Christian Roses Geistliche
> Schauspiele.* Berlin, 1913, pp. 41 and ff.
> and C. T. Gädertz : *Das niederdeutsche Drama.* Berlin,
> 1884, vol. I, p. 55.
> The only extant copy of this edition is in the Preussische
> Staatsbibliothek, Berlin. (Y q 4591).

39. 1650. *Judith Herois Tragoedia.* Das ist : Sigreiche Keuschheit der Heyligen und Wunderthätigen Heldin Judith. Welche 707 Jahr vor Christi Geburt, wider den Assyrischen Kriegsfürsten Holofernem, zu rettung des wahren Glaubens, und grösten Heyl dess damahlen hochbetrangten Vatterlands, hat obgesiget, und dem unreinen von Wein angefüllten Tyrannen, in seinem Beth, mit seiner Wehr, den Kopff abgeschlagen, allen Unkeuschen, so offt unversehens von Gott zeitlich, allzeit aber ewig gestrafft werden, nicht weniger zum Schrecken, als zur anmahnung aller keuschen Hertzen solcher schönen Tugend, nit ohne vergwisste Hoffnung dess ewigen Sigkräntzleins, biss in Todt beständig und starckmühtig nachzusetzen.

 Fürgestellt Von den Studiosis Soc. Jesu zu Lucern den 28. Augusti Anno 1650.

 Gedruckt zu Lucern, bey David Hautten. 4° pp. 12° .

 Programme. Latin and German. 12 pp. in 4°. Engelberg. Klosterbibliothek. (Sign. H. P. 392 " Miscellanea ").

 v. Backer-Sommervogel : *op. cit.* vol. V (1894) col. 160-161. (under Lucerne).

 J. Ehret : *Das Jesuitentheater zu Freiburg in der Schweiz* (I. Teil) Freiburg i /Brg. 1921, p. 197.

40. 1650. *Judith.* Acted on Aug. 28th 1650 in Luzern. Latin drama. MS. Engelberg. Klosterbibliothek. (Sign. " Judith, saec. 17. Nr. 368 ".) 128 pp. [1]

 v. Joseph Ehret : *Das Jesuitentheater zu Freiburg in der Schweiz* (I. Teil). Freiburg i /Brg. 1921, p. 194.

41. 1654. *Juditha et Holofernes.* Tragico-comoedia. Das ist Wunderbarlicher und frewdenreicher Sig der Gottsförchtigen und keuschen Judith : schmächlicher unnd schändlicher undergang dess stoltzen, grawsamen, Gottlosen Tyrannen Holofernis.

 Vorgestellt von der Jugend dess Churfürstlichen Gymnasij der Societet Jesu zu Landshuet. Den 3. Septemb. anno 1654. Getruckt zu München, bey Lucas Straub. 4°. 4 Bl.

 Programme of Jesuit academic drama.

 (Copy in Staatsbibliothek, München, Periochae I-M. Bavar. 2197. III. f. 52.)

 v. *Intermédiaire*, Paris, 1881. 10 Oct., col. 637.

 Serapeum Jahrgang XXVI (No. 5) Leipzig. 15. March, 1865, p. 79.

 Rothschild : *op. cit.* vol. V, p. cxxij.

 Backer-Sommervogel : *op. cit.* vol. IV, (1893), col. 1471 (under Landshut).

---

1. I am indebted to the courtesy of the librarian of the Engelberger Klosterbibliothek for permission to examine this MS.

42. 1663. *Holofernes.* A Puppet Play, acted in 1663.

> v. Samuel Pepys : *Diary* Aug. 6th 1663 : " A puppet play
> in Lincolnes Inn Fields, where there was the story of Holo-
> fernes, and other clockwork, well done ". (*Diary of Samuel
> Pepys.* ed. H. B. Wheatley, London, 1913, vol. III, p. 225.)

43. 1665. *Actio de Juditha.* Performed at the Gymnasium Josephinum, Hildesheim, on Sept. 15, 1665.

> v. R. Müller : *op. cit.* p. 57. with reference to *Liber com-
> plectens res gymnasii Hildesiensis Societatis Jesu ab ineunte
> anno 1654.* 2 vols. in folio (Gymnasialbibl : des Josephin-
> ums) [under 1665.] The passage to which reference is made
> is as follows :—15. (Dië) Veneris : Mane hora 7â omnes
> audiverunt sacrum, ut actores haberent tempus conqui-
> rendi vestes et theatrum ornari posset. A prandio actio
> de Juditha ; coepta paulo post primam ; duravit tribus
> horis cum distributione praemiorum. Bene successit.
> Vesperi in coena datus est scyphus vini P[1] Praefecto, M°
> Rhetorices, qui exhibuerat actionem, et praefecto chori
> musici. [1]
>
> (The passage in the *Liber* is the only evidence for this
> play.
>
> v. Müller : loc. cit. and p. 56.)
> [B. Duhr, *op. cit.* vol. III, 494, mentions a *Judith* acted
> in 1692 at Hildesheim ; there is no trace of this however
> in Müller's list of titles ; while the *Juditha* of 1665 is not
> mentioned in Duhr's work. Possibly the play acted in
> 1689 (No 49) may correspond to that mentioned by Duhr.]
> No further trace of either play is to be found in any
> library in Hildesheim. [2]

44. 1676. Fiducia victrix sive *Judith* de Holoferne triumphans ab
academ. juventute archiducalis collegii, et universitatis societatis Jesu Graecii dum consueta munificentia augustissimi
Romanorum imperatoris Leopoldi studiosae juventuti...
(Admont Stift Bibliothek)

> v. Richard Peinlich : *Geschichte des Gymnasiums in
> Graz.* 2te Periode. in *Jahresbericht des K. K. Ober-Gym-
> nasiums zu Graz 1869.* Graz, 1869, p. 85. (VI " Verzeich-
> nis der Schriften von Jesuiten und deren Schülern von
> 1553-1773 zu Graz durch den Druck veröffentlicht ".)
> and Backer-Sommervogel : *op. cit.* vol. IX (1900) col.
> 434 (under Gratz).

---

1. I am indebted to the kindness of the Director of the Gymnasium Josephinum
in Hildesheim for the transcription of this passage.

2. The authorities of the Stadtbücherei, Hildesheim, kindly supplied this information.

45. 1676. Am Rosenkranzsonntag bei der Prozession : *Geschichte der Judith* als scena muta. (at Einsiedeln).

> v. P. G. Morel in *Der Geschichtsfreund.* Mittheilungen des historischen Vereins der fünf Orte. vol. XVII, Einsiedeln etc. 1861, p. 103.

46. 1679. *Victrix fiducia Bethuliae.* Sigreiches Vertrawen auff Gott. In der Jüdischen Statt Bethulia, durch wunderbarliche Hülff Gottes von dem Undergang errettet. Vorgestelt von dem Churfürstlichen Gymnasio der Soc : Jesu zu München. Den 1. u. 5. Septembris, anno 1679. Getruckt bey Lucas Straub. 4°. 6 Bl. (Staatsbibliothek, München, 2 copies : 1) Periochae 1670-1679 Bavar. 2193 III. 70. 2) Periochae Bavar. 2195 I. 34.)

> Programme of Jesuit academic drama.
>
> v. *Intermédiaire.* Paris, 1881. 10 Oct., col. 637.
>
> *Serapeum* XXVI. (No. 23) Leipzig. 15 Dec. 1865, p. 368.
>
> Rothschild : *op. cit.* vol. V, p. cxxij.
>
> K. von Reinhardstöttner : *Zur Geschichte des Jesuitendramas in München* in *Jahrbuch für Münchener Geschichte* 3. Jahrgang. Bamberg, 1889, p. 118. (cites Sept. lst. 5th and 6th).
>
> also P. Bernhard Duhr. S. J. *op. cit.* vol. III. (München, 1921) p. 467, where *Judith* is said to have been performed in 1678 *and* 1679.

47. 1681. *Von Judith der Grossmüthigen,* in J. Hoefel : *Historisches Gesangbuch.* Schleusingen, 1681, p. 365 (and ff.)

> A narrative poem of didactic character, consisting of 31 stanzas. (copy in British Museum).

48. 1684. *Die Geschichte von Judith und Holofernes.* Acted on Aug. 20th 1684. at Einsiedeln.

> v. P. G. Morel : loc. cit. (pp. 105-106).

49. 1689. Das / Durch *Judith* von seinem unbilligen und gewaltsamen Verfolger HOLOFERNE / endlich / Erlösete / BETHULIEN, / Wie / Dasselbe in etwas Umständlicher betrach / tet, und in einem geringen Schau=Spiel : nebst an / muhtiger *Music* vorgestellet, / Und / Zu Gottes Ehren, auch Übung der Deutschen / Mutter-Sprache, samt wolanständigen / Sitten, / Nicht / weniger / Zu nützlicher Erinnerung vieler erbaulichen / Lehren, bey diesen gefährlichen / und traurigen Zeiten / Ohne üppigen Pracht, nach Zeit und Orts / Gelegenheit, / Durch / Einige *Alumnos* des Gymnasii Andreani / alter Stadt Hildesheim, /Den 8 und 9 Octobr. 1689, geliebts Gott, auff / eines Hoch=Edlen Rahts Reit=Stall soll / vorgestellet werden / Von / J. C. LOSIO / RECTORE, Hildesheim, gedruckt bey Michael

Geissmarn.   6 Bl. 4º. Sign. A2-B u. 12 S. V Actus (Inhalts-angabe) mit Gesängen, Tänzen und Zwischenspiel von Moroso-phus und Virlefix.

Schluss.   Vorstellung der gesammten Agenten.

EPILOGUS.   Der Frantzösische Bauren = Tantz. Nach= Spiel.

v. K. Th. Gaedertz : *Archivalische Nachrichten* ed. cit. (Anmerkungen), p. 129.

This play is not preserved in any library in Hildesheim. [1]

50. 1691. *Fastus confusus seu a Juditha fusus Holofernus.* 4o. P. Vitus Kaltenkranter e S. Petro. (music by Henricus Biber Salisb. Cap. mag.) Joanni Ernesto electo Archiepisc. dedicatum. Salzburg. 28 Nov. 1691.

Programme. (Latin and German). Copy in the Öffent-liche Studienbibliothek, Salzburg. (4003. I).

v. also H. F. Wagner : *op. cit.* pp. 270-1. and p. 328.

51. 1693. *Victrix fiducia Bethuliae.*   Sigreiches Vertrawen auf Gott, der sehr wundersam erretteten Stadt Bethulia, Durch die dapffer-und Helden-mässige Judith.   Vorgestellt von der Cath-olisch-studierenden Jugend, in dem Gymnasio der Soc : Jesu zu Augspurg, bey S. Salvator.   Den 2. u. 4. Herbstmonats im Jahr 1693. Augspurg, gedruckt bey Maria Magdalena Utz-schneiderin.   4o.   4 Bl.

Programme.   Copy in Staatsbibliothek, München (Pe-riochae Bavar. 2193. V. 28.) and in Stadtbibliothek, Augs-burg (Gymnasium St. Salvator, 4o. Aug.).

Except in the wording of the sub-title, this periocha is verbally identical with No. 47. and obviously represents the same drama.   Printing, page-division, and of course the list of actors, differ from those of the Munich programme.

v. *Intermédiaire*, Paris, 1881. 10 Oct., col. 637.

and Backer-Sommervogel : *op. cit.* vol. I (1890), col. 655. (under Augsburg).

52. 1693. *Bethulias Rettung durch Judith.* Acted at the Jesuit College in Augsburg, in 1693. " Gedruckt von Maria Magda-lena Utzschneiderin. "   Probably the same drama as No. 51.

v. E. Weller ; *Annalen*, ed. cit. vol. II, p. 289.

and P. Bahlmann : *Das Drama der Jesuiten* in *Euphorion* vol. II. (Bamberg, 1895) p. 278.

53. 1701. *Judith mit Holofernes.* Acted 15. Aug. at Einsiedeln " auf den kleinern [Theater] : Jahel und Sisara, als Vorbilder, theils in stummer Szene, theils in Gespräch und Gesang ".

v. P. G. Morel : loc. cit. (pp. 112-113).

---

1. This statement is based on information kindly supplied by the authorities of the Stadtbücherei, Hildesheim.

54. 1704. *Die Heldenmüthige Judith* in einem teutschen Oratorio. Performed at Vienna 27 July, 1704. Composed by J. M. Zächer.

> v. A. von Weilen : *Zur Theatergeschichte Wiens* (Schriften des österreichischen Vereins für Bibliothekswesen), Wien, 1901, p. 64. (Copy in Nationalbibliothek, Wien. No 406. 773-B).

55. 1708. Am Rosenkranzsonntag. Stumme Scenen aus der Geschichte der *Judith*. Acted at Einsiedeln.

> v. P. G. Morel : loc. cit. (p. 113).

56. 1714. *Judith sua in Deum fiducia de Holoferne triumphans* exhibita a .. Juliae Juventute. Anno 1714, 27 Sept. Coloniae Agrippinae, typis Caspari Drimborn. 4o. Lat. u. deutsch (Darsteller : 22 ex Rhetorica, 8 ex Poetica, 5 ex Syntaxi, 4 ex Secunda, 4 ex Infima, 3 ex Tyrocinio).

> Programme.

> v. P. Bahlmann : *Jesuitendramen der niederrheinischen Ordensprovinz* in *Centralblatt für Bibliothekswesen*. Beiheft XV (in vol. VI) Leipzig, 1896-7, p. 60.

> and Backer-Sommervogel : *op. cit.* vol. IX (1900), col. 527. (under Juliers).

57. 1720. *Judithae de Holoferne Iustitiae de Impietate Triumphus*. Lusus tragico-comicus ab Electorali Gymnasio P. P. Soc : Jesu Heidelberga Scenis Autumnalibus in Theatrum datus, Quando Serenissimus ac potentissimus Princeps ac Dominus D. Carolus Philippus, Comes Palatinus ad Rhenum S.R. j. Archithesaurarius et Elector... Dominus ac Meccenas Noster Clementissimus Victoriosis in Arena Litteraria Palaestritis Virtutis et Doctrinae praemia Electorali munificentiâ gratiosissimè elargiebatur. In Aula Majore Gymnasii P. P. Soc : Jesu Anno â partu Virginis 1720 Calend. Octobr. MS. in Staatsbibliothek, München. Cod. lat. 1693.

> v. Backer-Sommervogel : *op. cit.* vol. IV, 210. (under Heidelberg).

58. 1720. Joachim Beccau : *L'Amor insanguinato* oder *Holofernes*, in einem Singspiel.

> v. J. Beccau : *Theatralische Gedichte und Übersetzungen.* Hamburg, 1720.

> An opera, with arias in both Italian and German, and comic scenes in dialect.

> v. Goedeke : *Grundriss* : ed. cit. vol. III, p. 337.
> Gottsched : *Nöthiger Vorrath* ed. cit. vol. I, p. 293.
> and Rothschild : *op. cit.* vol. V, p. CLJ.

59. 1722. *Judith und Holofernes.* Produced at Riga in November,
1722, by the actor-manager J. H. Mann for the benefit of the
hospital of S. Georg.

> v. Riga Stadtarchiv, *Ratsarchiv, Publica* vol. 83, p. 318.
> "Protokoll vom 21 Nov. 1722", where the following pas-
> sage occurs : Es sollen die Comœdianten heute über acht
> Tagen, besagten Armen zum besten gegen Abkürtzung
> derer ihnen einmahl nachgegebenen und für die Wache
> und Licht zu verwendenden Kosten von Judith und
> Holofernus (*sic*) zu agiren und solches durch die gewöhn-
> liche Zettullen jedermänniglich bekanndt zu machen
> gehalten seyn. [1]. v. also J. Bolte : *Das Danziger Theater im
> 16. und 17. Jahrhundert.* (*Theatergeschichtliche Forschungen*
> XII.) Hamburg und Leipzig, 1895, p. 161 (note 3).

60. (ca.) 1725. *Judithae de Holopherne Triumphus.* A " carmen "
in F. le Jay S. J. *Bibliotheca Rhetorum* praecepta et exempla
complectens quae ad poeticam facultatem pertinent, discipulis
pariter ac magistris perutilis.. Ingolstadt, 1725, vol. IV, p. 181.

61. 1732. *Siege of Bethulia.* Performed at Bartholomew's Fair, on
Lee and Harper's stage. Engravings were made of a scene
from this show.

> v. H. Morley : *Memoirs of Bartholomew Fair.* London,
> 1859. pp. 394-5.
> and William Hone : *Everyday Book.* London, 1826,
> vol. I, (Pt. II) col. 1223-1227 (where the date is given as
> 1721, an error corrected by H. Morley, *loc. cit.*)

62. 1732. J. G. Haman : *Judith.*
> An opera, written for the Hamburg theatre.
> v. Rothschild : *op. cit.* vol. V, p. CLJ.
> and H. M. Schletterer : *Das deutsche Singspiel von
> seinen ersten Anfängen bis auf die neueste Zeit.* Augsburg,
> 1863, p. 210.

63. 1733. *Judith.* An oratorio or sacred drama by W... H... Esq.,
the music composed by W. de la Fesch. (Copy in the British
Museum).

64. 1743. *Firma in Deum fiducia maxima Regnorum tutela, in Judith
Bethuliae vindice.* Drama sub Mariae Theresiae in Reginam
Bohemiae coronatae solemnia. Prag, 1743.

---

1. I am indebted to the kindness of the Librarian of the Stadtbibliothek, Riga
(Dr. N. Busch), for the transcription of this passage from the town archives, and
for the further information that the actors received 4 Taler for their expenses from
a previous performance of the comedy *Vom reichen Mann und armen Lazaro* (like-
wise produced for the benefit of the hospital), and that the plays produced by
Mann's company in the previous year included " Tartiff " and " Lür " (*Tartuffe*
and (?) *Lear*).

Programme of Jesuit academic drama, by P. Ferd. Silbermann.

v. *Intermédiaire*. Paris, 1881, 10 Oct., col. 638.

Backer-Sommervogel : *op. cit.* vol. VI (1895), col. 1164 (under Prague) and VII (1896), col. 1206. (under Silbermann).

65. 1754. *Die über Holofernes obsiegende Judith* : vorgestellet von einer... Jugend der 5ten Schule bey denen P. P. der Gesellschafft Jesu binnen Düsseldorf d. 25. u. 26. Herbst-monath 1754... Gedruckt (in Düsseldorf) bey der Wittib Tilm. 4 Bl. 4o. Deutsch. Mit dem Text der Gesänge. Die Täntz hat eingerichtet Monsieur Simons. Darsteller aus der 5 (24), 2(4) und 1(1) Schule. Reliquos scena dabit.

Programme of Jesuit academic drama.

v. P. Bahlmann : *Jesuitendramen der niederrheinischen Ordensprovinz* in *Centralblatt für Bibliothekswesen*, Beiheft XV (in vol. VI) Leipzig, 1896-7, p. 34.

and Backer-Sommervogel : *op. cit.* vol. IX (1900), col. 260 (under Duesseldorf).

66. 1755. Ein Comödia, oder christliches Schauspihll von dem Arphaxat, ein Künig der Medyer : und auch von der heldenmüothigen *Judith*, wie selbe den Holofernem überwunden.

MS., in three acts, dating from 1755, and written by Mathias Schmidli in Ruswil, in the possession of a family in the canton of Luzern.

v. Rothschild : *op. cit.* vol. V, p. CLIJ.

and A. Lütolf : *Aus der frühen Schaubühne der Stadt und Landschaft Luzern* : in *Mitteilungen des historischen Vereins der fünf Orte* in *Geschichtsfreund* XXIII (Einsiedeln) 1868, pp. 186-202, where extracts are printed. From these it is evident that this drama is in the main copied from the *Tragoedia Mundi* of 1647 (No. 37).

[The first extract is a verbally exact copy of II, 9, the scene of the banquet, until for the short "cantus" in the MS. of *Tragoedia Mundi* a long comic dialogue is substituted. The other extracts correspond except in details]. A "vivat Lucerna" is inserted in the final scene, to remind Luzern of her leadership in Catholic Switzerland ; Judith is evidently meant to represent Luzern.

67. 1761. *Judith*, a Sacred Drama, with music by Dr. Arne.

Performed at the Theatre Royal in Drury Lane in 1761 ; the text was printed that year and also three years later, when the work was performed at the Lock Hospital Chapel. (Copies of both issues in the British Museum).

68. 1760-1770 (?) *Judith und Holofernes.* Volksschauspiel.
MS. in the Steiermärkisches Landesarchiv, Graz.
Published in Anton Schlossar : *Deutsche Volksschauspiele.*
In Steiermark gesammelt. 2 vols. Halle, 1891. (vol. II,
pp. 1-38).

69. 1763. *Judith.* Tragoedia Reverendissimo, Perillustri, Amplissi-
moque Viro ac Domino Domino Gabrieli Hilgers, sacri, canonici, ac exempti ordinis Praemonstratensis, Ecclesiae Steinfeldensis Abbati... dicata, acta ludis autumnalibus ab ingenua,
praenobili, lectissimaque Juventute Gymnadis Mariae-Lauretanae Fratrum Minorum S. Francisci Conventualium Monjaviae diebus 26 et 27 Septembris 1763. Aquisgrani.
This programme of a Franciscan scholastic drama contains a German scenarium and German text of songs, as
well as the names of the scholars acting the parts. It is
in the Aachener Stadtbibliothek. (v. Appendix B.).
v. *Zeitschrift des Aachener Geschichtsvereins*, Aachen,
1902, vol. XXIV, p. 553.

70. 1770. *Die heldenmütige Judit.* " Volksschauspiel " performed
at Afing, Sarntal, Tirol.
v. Adalbert Sikora : *Zur Geschichte der Volksschauspiele
in Tirol.* in *Zeitschrift des Ferdinandeums* l. c. (p. 371).

71. 1771. Isaac Pfaler : *Die heldenmuthige Jüdin oder Judith*, ein
Trauerspiel. Nürnberg, 1771.
v. Goedeke ; *Grundriss* ed. cit. Bd. V, II, p. 357.
and Rothschild : *op. cit.* vol. V, p. CLIJ.

72. 1772. *Judith.* Ein Heldengedichte. Leipzig, 1772. (Gedruckt
bey Johann Friedrich Langenheim. A narrative poem, written,
with indifferent skill, in 8-foot lines rhyming in couplets.
(A prayer and a song of Judith are in lyric stanzas).
v. Goedeke : *Grundriss*, ed. cit. Bd. IV, p. 124 (where
the date is given as 1773). In Universitätsbibliothek,
Leipzig. Litt. germ. 30104. [1]

73. 1776. J. W. L. Gleim : *Vierzeiler auf Judith* in Poetische Blu-
menlese auf das Jahr 1776 (Göttinger Musenalmanach), p. 76.

74. 1785. *Judith und Holofernes.* Puppet play acted at Hamburg
in 1785.
v. H. M. Schletterer : *Das deutsche Singspiel, von seinen
ersten Anfängen bis auf die neueste Zeit.* Augsburg,
1863, p. 229.
v. also Flögels *Geschichte des Grotesk-Komischen* (ed.F. W.
Ebeling). Leipzig 1862, pp. 206 and 211.]

---

1. By the kindness of the authorities of the Universitätsbibliothek, Leipzig,
this copy was lent to me for examination.

75. 1798. *Judith.* " Melodrama. Musik von Johann Fuss. " Press-
burg, 1798.

> v. Rothschild : *op. cit.* vol. V, p. CLIJ.
> Clément et Larousse : *Dictionnaire lyrique.* Paris, 1869,
> etc., p. 386.
> and H. Riemann : *Opernhandbuch.* Leipzig, 1887,
> p. 252. (where the composer is cited as *Georg* Fuss).

76. 1799. *Judith.* " Grosse Oper. Musik von Leopold Kozeluch ".
Produced at Vienna ca. 1799.

> v. Rothschild : *op. cit.* vol. V, p. CLIJ.
> Clément et Larousse : *op. cit.* p. 386.
> and H. Riemann : *op. cit.,* p. 252.

77. ca. 1800. *Judith.* Oratorio by Joseph Emmert, performed at
Würzburg.

> v. H. Riemann : *op. cit.,* p. 252.

78. 1809. " Heinrich von Itzenloe " (i.e. Heinrich Keller, of Zürich)
Judith. Schauspiel von H. von Itzenloe, Hofpoet bey Kaiser
Rudolf II. Aus einer alten Handschrift. Zürich, 1809.
A Romantic drama.

> v. Goedeke : *Grundriss* : ed. cit. Bd. VI, p. 471.
> B. Wyss : *Heinrich Keller.* Der Züricher Bildhauer und
> Dichter. Frauenfeld, 1891, pp. 49-50.
> and J. Grimm in *Kleinere Schriften* vol. VI (Rezensionen
> und Vermischte Aufsätze III. Theil) Berlin, 1882. pp. 9 ff.

79. 1818. *Judith und Holofernes.* Ein Drama in 5 Akten. Zerbst,
1818.

> v. Rothschild : *op. cit.* vol. V, p. clij.
> and C. G. Kayser : *Deutsche Bücherkunde.* Leipzig, 1825-7,
> II. Theil, Anhang, p. 181.
> (Copy in Preussische Staatsbibliothek, Berlin.   Ys 3971ª).

80. 1824. Carl Weisflog : *Der wüthende Holofernes* in *Phantasiestücke
und Historien.* Bd. I, (Dresden, 1824) pp. 85-100.

81. 1825. J. F. Pennie : *The Fair Avenger,* or *The Destroyer destroyed.*
" An academic drama ". London, 1825. (Published together
with *Scenes in Palestine* or *Dramatic Sketches from the Bible*).
(Copy in British Museum).

82. (ca.) 1830. *Judith.* Oratorio by Joseph Strauss. Performed
at Karlsruhe. v. H. Riemann : *op. cit.* p. 252.

83. 1841. *Judith.* Oratorio by K. Eckert. Performed at Berlin.
28 Jan. 1841. v. H. Riemann : *op. cit.* p. 252.

84. 1841. Friedrich Hebbel : *Judith*. Hamburg, 1841.
    v. F. Hebbel : *Sämtliche Werke*. herausgeg. R. M. Werner. Berlin, 1901-03. vol. I, pp. 1-81.
    also Hebbel : *Briefe* (*Sämtliche Werke* 3. Abteilung). ed. R. M. Werner. vol. II, Berlin, 1905, pp. 23-37.
    Judith. Ein Trauerspiel in 3 Akten. was printed " als Manuscript " in 1840. v. H. Wütschke : *Hebbel-Bibliographie*. Berlin, 1910, pp. 18 and 19. The drama was first performed on July 6. 1840 at the Berlin Hoftheater.

85. 1847. J. Nestroy : *Judith und Holofernes*.
    A one-act parody of Hebbel's drama.
    v. J. Nestroy : *Gesammelte Werke* herausgeg. V. Chiavacci u. L. Ganghofer. Lieferung 36. Stuttgart, 1891. (pp. 241-259).

86. 1849. *Judith* or *The Prophetess of Bethulia*. A Romance from the Apocrypha. London, 1849.
    A prose tale giving the apocryphal story.
    (Copy in British Museum).

87. 1854. *Judith, or an old Picture of Absolutism re-touched*. London 1854.
    A short narrative poem.
    (Copy in British Museum).

88. 1856. J. M. Neale : *Judith*. A Seatonian Prize Poem. Cambridge, 1856.
    v. J. M. Neale : *Seatonian Poems*. Cambridge, 1864.
    and *Letters of John Mason Neale*. Selected and edited by his daughter (Mary Sackville Lawson). London, 1910, p. 279.

89. 1858. *Judith*. Grosse Oper in drei Aufzügen. Musik von Emil Naumann.
    Performed at Dresden 5 Nov. 1858.
    v. H. Riemann : *op. cit.* p. 252.
    Rothschild : *op. cit.* vol. V, p. CLIIJ.
    and Clément et Larousse : *op. cit.* p. 386.
    Possibly this is the opera to which Hebbel refers in a letter to Christine Hebbel of June 23. 1858 : " Eine Oper " Judith ", ganz nach meinem Stück, kommt nächstens zur Aufführung ". v. *Briefe* ed. cit. vol. VI (Berlin, 1906) Nr. 610, p. 152. (Music to Hebbel's *Judith* had already been composed in 1851 by Julius Rietz. v. H. Riemann : *op. cit.* p. 252).

90. 1858. *Judith*. Biblical cantata ; the words selected from Holy Scriptures by Henry F. Chorley and the music composed by Henry Leslie.

This cantata was written for the Birmingham Musical Festival in 1858 and sold for the benefit of the General Hospital.
(Copy in British Museum).

91. 1869. Julius Grosse : Iambic version of Hebbel's *Judith*. In *Gesammelte dramatische Werke*. Leipzig, 1870. vol. VII. pp. 1-106.

v. J. W. Grosse : *Ursachen und Wirkungen*. Lebenserinnerungen. Braunschweig, 1896. p. 418, and pp. 422-3.
" Hebbels Judith ". Beilage Allgemeine Zeitung 1901. Nr. 300.
and R. M. Werner : *Julius Grosses Judith*. Ein Beitrag zur Geschichte des Hebbelschen Dramas. Prager Deutsche Studien vol. IX. II. Teil. Prag, 1908.

92. 1870. *Judith*. Grosse Oper in vier Akten. by A. Fr. Doppler (text by J. Mosenthal). Performed at Vienna 30. Dec. 1870.

v. H. Riemann : *op. cit*. p. 252.
(Copy in Nationalbibliothek, Wien. Nº 112 F 103).

93. 1887. *Judith*. " heroic opera " by M. F. Moelle, with music by Carl Goetze.
Performed at Magdeburg in 1887.

v. Clément et Larousse : *Dictionnaire des Opéras*. (Dictionnaire lyrique) revu... par A. Pougin. Paris, 1898. p. 624.

94. 1891. *Judith und Holofernes*. Lyric drama performed at Boston in 1891 by the United Hebrew Opera Company (the programmes being in Hebrew and the opera being sung in German).

v. Clément et Larousse : *Dictionnaire des Opéras* ed. cit. p. 624.

95. 1896. Thomas Bailey Aldrich : *Judith and Holofernes*. Boston and New York, 1896.
A narrative poem in blank verse.

v. F. Greenslet : *Life of Thomas Bailey Aldrich*. London (Boston and New York) 1908. (pp. 69-71, 228-231, and 278).

96. 1904. T. B. Aldrich : *Judith of Bethulia*. A tragedy. Boston and New York, 1904.
A dramatisation of the narrative poem (No. 95).

v. Greenslet : *op. cit*. p. 228.

97. 1911. T. Sturge Moore : *Judith*.
A one-act poetic play, published in 1911, and performed by the Stage Society in 1916.

v. *The Observer*. 30. Jan. 1916.
and *The Sunday Times*. 30. Jan. 1916.

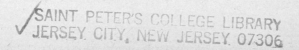

98. 1911.　Georg Kaiser : *Die jüdische Witwe.*　Bühnenspiel in fünf Akten. Berlin, 1911.

99. 1915.　Otto Burchard : *Judith und Holofernes.*　Ein patriotisches Schauspiel in fünf Aufzügen.　Frankfurt a /M. 1915.

100. 1918.　C. Gondlach : *Judith.*　Eine Erzählung aus vorchristlicher Zeit.　Mainz, 1918.

101. 1918.　Sebastian Wieser : *Judith.*　Schauspiel in 5 Akten (für Freilichtbühne) Rastatt 1918. (2te Auflage, Regensburg, 1919).

102. 1919.　Arnold Bennett : *Judith.*　A Play in Three Acts.　Founded on the Apocryphal book of Judith.　London, 1919. Performed at Eastbourne in April, 1919 [1].

103. 1921.　Rosmarie Menschick : *Judith.*　Biblisches Schauspiel in 4 Aufzügen mit nur weiblichen Rollen.　München, 1921.

ADDENDA TO CHRONOLOGICAL SURVEY

1863.　Rudolf Kulemann : *Judith.* Epos. Dresden, 1863.
v. K. L. Leimbach : *Die Deutschen Dichter der Neuzeit und Gegenwart.* vol. V. Leipzig. Frankfurt a. M. [1893] pp. 208 and 219.

1876.　A. Schmitz : *Judith.*　Trauerspiel. [Leipzig], 1876.
v. A. Krüger : *Literaturlexikon.*　München, 1914. (under Schmitz) p. 389, col. 1.

1887.　Wolfgang Arthur Jordan : *Judith, die Löwin Judas.*　Narrative poem (published in the Tilsiter Zeitung 1887).
v. K. L. Leimbach : *op. cit.* vol. IV, Kassel, 1890. pp. 120-126.

---

1. It is announced that Mr. Eugene Goossens is engaged upon an opera, based on Mr. Arnold Bennett's play of *Judith.* (*Westminster Gazette.* 19 Sept. 1925).

II

THE TREATMENT OF THE JUDITH STORY

If number and variety of versions, widespread and enduring popularity, be any criterion of greatness, the tale of Judith, it must be conceded, is one of the great stories of the world's literature. From the ninth century to the present day, as is apparent from the foregoing chronological list of versions, it has exercised a curious fascination over the minds of poets and dramatists in Germany and England. Nor is this popularity confined to the Germanic peoples, though it is, on the whole, earlier evident amongst them. Later, Romance treatments are just as frequent, and their importance is not inconsiderable [1]. Even allowing for the paramount influence of biblical tradition, such as would contribute to the early popularity of any tale with Scriptural authority behind it, there is some warrant for supposing that the story itself contained elements of unusual interest, appealed with special point to the audiences of earlier days, and to the writers of a later age.

On consideration, indeed, we find the Apocryphal story has two of the essentials of a great tale. It has dramatic moments. It embodies a great idea. Moreover, the setting is picturesque, capable of adaptation to the needs of a particular environment ; the characters and action provide scope for contrast, dramatic suspense, enthusiasm.

Calamity, in the shape of a conquering tyrant, has suddenly befallen the Hebrew race. Holofernes, the emissary of Nabuchodonosor, is a mighty warrior before whom even the strongest have submitted ; and in his anger at the resistance of the small Jewish race, he has vowed to exterminate the nation that shall be the last to surrender to him. Bethulia is besieged by the armies of Holofernes, encamped on the surrounding plain, and is in the last

---

1. It is interesting to note that the latest version of the story is an opera by Arthur Honegger (a composer of the French school and of Swiss parentage) performed at Mézières, Switzerland in the summer of 1925.

stages of misery and despair. Some counsel surrender, hoping thereby to avoid certain death; others regard death as inevitable, the fate of God's chosen people as sealed. The message of God, however, comes to Judith, widow of Manasses; she comforts the people and bids them endure for five days more, while she goes out in all her beauty to the camp of Holofernes. There with cunning words she deceives him, telling him that the Jews can never be overcome until they sin against their God, and promising to lead him to Jerusalem when (through prayer in the valley by night) she has learnt that they have eaten the firstfruits of the Lord and sinned against Him. Overcome by her beauty and her eloquence, Holofernes gives orders that she shall be housed and allowed to pass in and out of the camp to pray. On the fourth day, a feast is prepared, to which Holofernes bids her come; after drinking deeply he is left lying on his bed within the tent, where only Judith remains. She takes his faulchion from above his head and smites him twice and kills him. She and her maid then pass out, as is their custom, and bear back the tyrant's head to Bethulia, where it is hung high upon the walls. In the morning the Jews sally out against the Assyrians, who, when they discover Holofernes dead, flee and are utterly vanquished. Then Judith sings a thanksgiving to the Lord before all Israel; and returns to her house, where she grows old and dies, honoured throughout the land.

The Apocryphal book early provides religious art with an effective subject. Much could be written on the representation of Judith in Art; but this is in itself a large theme, and falls outside the scope of the present study [1]. Two pictures, however, have inspired two literary descriptions of such excellence and insight that these may well be quoted as preface to a discussion of the Judith story in literature. The first is Heine's description of the *Judith* of Horace Vernet; the second, more famous passage occurs in Ruskin's *Mornings in Florence,* where he speaks of 'Sandro's Small Judith'. Both seize the dramatic quality which the painter has perceived in the central figure; but Heine, describing a more modern picture, gives an imaginative view of Judith's character, while Ruskin, dealing with a work of early religious art, seizes the great idea behind the portrait. 'She is returning', he says, 'to the camp of her Israel, followed by her maid carrying the head of Holofernes. And she

---

1. Cp. an interesting article on this subject by Professor Dr. Ed. Heyck, in *Über Land und Meer.* 50. Jahrgang, Bd. 99, Nr. 1. (1908).

walks in one of Botticelli's light dancing actions, her drapery all on flutter....... Do you happen to know anything about Judith yourself, except that she cut off Holofernes' head ; and has been made the high light of about a million vile pictures ever since ?...... Now, as in many other cases of noble history, apocryphal or other, I do not in the least care how far the literal facts are true. The conception of facts, and the idea of Jewish womanhood, are there, grand and real as a marble statue — possession for all ages. And you will feel, after you have read this piece of history, or epic poetry, with honourable care, that there is somewhat more to be thought of and pictured in Judith, than painters have mostly found it in them to shew you : that she is not merely the Jewish Dalilah to the Assyrian Samson, but the mightiest, purest, brightest type of high passion in severe womanhood offered to our human memory. Sandro's picture is but slight : but it is true to her, and the only one I know that is ; and after writing out these verses, you will see why he gives her that swift, peaceful motion, while you read in her face only sweet solemnity of dreaming thought. 'My people delivered, and by my hand ; and God has been gracious to his handmaid !' The triumph of Miriam over a fallen host, the fire of an exulting mortal life in an immortal hour, the purity and severity of a guardian angel — all are here..... ' [1].

Heine's description of Horace Vernet's painting is of a very different order :

'Das vorzüglichste seiner ausgestellten Gemälde war eine Judith, die im Begriff steht, den Holofernes zu töten. Sie hat sich eben vom Lager desselben erhoben, ein blühend schlankes Mädchen. Ein violettes Gewand, um ihre Hüften hastig geschürzt, geht bis zu ihren Füssen hinab ; oberhalb des Leibes trägt sie ein blassgelbes Unterkleid, dessen Ärmel von der rechten Schulter herunterfällt, und den sie mit der linken Hand, etwas metzgerhaft und doch zugleich bezaubernd zierlich, wieder in die Höhe streift ; denn mit der rechten Hand hat sie eben das krumme Schwert gezogen gegen den schlafenden Holofernes. Da steht sie, eine reizende Gestalt, an der eben überschrittenen Grenze der Jungfräulichkeit, ganz gottrein und doch weltbefleckt, wie eine entweihte Hostie. Ihr Kopf ist wunderbar anmutig und unheimlich liebenswürdig ; schwarze Locken, wie kurze Schlangen, die nicht herabflattern,

---

1. *Mornings in Florence* : Third Morning, in Ruskin : *Works*, ed. E. T. Cook and A. Wedderburn (Library Edition), vol. XXIII, pp. 335-7.

sondern sich bäumen, furchtbar graziös. Das Gesicht ist etwas beschattet und süsse Wildheit, düstere Holdseligkeit und sentimentaler Grimm rieselt durch die edlen Züge der tödlichen Schönen. Besonders in ihrem Auge funkelt süsse Grausamkeit und die Lüsternheit der Rache ; denn sie hat auch den eigenen beleidigten Leib zu rächen an dem hässlichen Heiden. In der Tat, dieser ist nicht sonderlich liebreizend, aber im Grunde scheint er doch bon enfant zu sein. Er schläft so gutmütig in der Nachwonne seiner Beseligung ; er schnarcht vielleicht, oder, wie Luise sagt, er schläft laut ; seine Lippen bewegen sich noch, als wenn sie küssten — er lag noch eben im Schosse des Glücks ; — und trunken von Glück und gewiss auch von Wein, ohne Zwischenspiel von Qual und Krankheit, sendet ihn der Tod durch seinen schönsten Engel in die weisse Nacht der ewigen Vernichtung. Welch ein beneidenswertes Ende ! wenn ich einst sterben soll, ihr Götter, lasst mich sterben wie Holofernes! Ist es Ironie von Horace Vernet, dass die Strahlen der Frühsonne auf den Schlafenden gleichsam verklärend hereinbrechen, und dass eben die Nachtlampe erlischt? [1].

It is characteristic of Heine — as indeed of the later, more sophisticated versions of the story — that the figure of Holofernes should occupy him, that he should find the dramatic interest in the interaction of the two characters. Characteristic also of a later age is the realisation of the complexity of motive behind Judith's deed. Not for Horace Vernet — nor for Heine — was the conception of a woman dominated and inspired by a sole motive, by the divine mission entrusted to her weakness. The spirit of the nineteenth century, as will be seen, refashioned the whole story in the light of this new psychological analysis. For earlier ages, however, the telling of the tale was not complicated by such considerations. The contrast was a simple one — that of a weak woman and a heathen warrior, with the might of the God of Israel (and of Christianity) aiding the weak. The supernatural element of the story is emphasised in the defeat of the man by the woman ; the attributes of womanhood are employed as the arm of the Lord to slay the heathen. A natural shrinking from the deed of violence is all that is conceded to Judith in the earlier versions — sometimes

---

1. Heine : *Französische Zustände* II (Gemäldeausstellung von 1831) in *Sämmtliche Werke*. vol. X, Hamburg, 1885, p. 155. It is of interest to note in this connection that Hebbel, when he saw Vernet's picture in Paris, recognised in it a conception akin to his own. (v. Letter to Elise Lensing 2. April 1844 in Hebbel : *Briefe* (*Sämtliche Werke* 3. Abteilung) ed. R. M. Werner, vol. III, Berlin 1905. Nr. 184, p. 67).

there is no trace even of this in the exalted faith of her prayer to the Almighty.   The dominance of the religious motive is complete.

The earliest English version of the story — the Old English poem *Judith* — is a heroic treatment of this religious theme.   Only the last three cantos of the poem have been preserved, but they contain the crisis of the story.   That the situation is already crucial is plain from the opening lines ; Judith is in the camp of the Assyrians and her faith is firm in God :

> . . . . . .   hēo þār þā gearwe funde
> mundbyrd aet þām māēran þēodne, þā hēo ahte māēste þearfe
> hyldo þæs hēhstan Dēman, þæt hē hīe wiþ þaes hēhstan brōgan
> gefriþode, frymþa Waldend ; . . . .

It is already the fourth day of her sojourn, and Holofernes has prepared a feast.   There follows a description of the feast — a theme congenial to the poet — and of its effect on Holofernes.   He is carried to his tent, whither Judith has been led to await him.   She prays to God, and with strength granted her from on high smites Holofernes twice, so that his head is severed from his body — and his soul, the poet adds, condemned to darkness.   All this takes place in the first of the three cantos.   The second is occupied with Judith's return to Bethulia, her advice to the people, and the great combat which ensues between the Israelites and the Assyrians. The poet dwells with delight on the details of the battle, the clashing of swords, the flight of arrows, the hurling of spears, and all the traditional heroic activity of epic poetry.   The descriptions of war are continued in the last canto, and the discovery of the death of Holofernes gives occasion for one of the elegiac laments common in the old alliterative epic.   Finally, tributes of arms and spoil are brought to Judith, as to all epic heroes, and the poet sings praises to the might of the Lord as he relates how she lays these offerings at His feet.

The treatment of the theme is epic rather than merely narrative. There is a breadth of imagination in it which, even more than the traditional epic form, entitles it to the higher claim.   'The fashioning grasp of imagination' (as a writer who is both poet and critic says of *Sigurd*) [1] ' has not only seized on the show of things, and not only on the physical and moral unity of things, but has somehow brought into the midst of all this... something of the ultimate and

---

1. Lascelles Abercrombie : *The Epic* (Art and Craft of Letters Series) p. 50,
The Story of Judith.

metaphysical significance of life'. The Old English poem does
attempt to narrate a great deed, and to relate it to the ultimate
problem of divine grace. The ideal of personal consecration —
an essential part of the Hebraic conception of life — is pourtrayed
in the heroic terms of a Germanic epic ; and it is this central
unifying idea which transforms the narrative of events into an
epic poem. Again and again it occurs, like a refrain :

> ' þe hēo ahte trumne gelēafan
> ā tō þām Aelmihtigan' ;
>
> Hī þā se hēhsta Dēma
> āēdre mid elne onbryrde' ;
>
> ' swā hyre God ūþe ' ;

Judith is characterised, in the epic manner, by fixed epithets ;
but they do not recall her beauty, save on rare occasions; they
emphasise the wisdom which comes from God. She is 'Metodes
mēowle', 'sēo hālige', 'þā snoteran idese', 'sēo snotere maegþ,' 'glēaw
on geþonce'. Her beauty is a secondary attribute, to be used by
the wisdom of God. Only in combination with 'glēaw on geþonce'
is she 'ides ælfscīnu' — when the poet notes that it was already
the fourth day after the 'virgin of elfin-bright beauty' had sought
Holofernes. Once, indeed, her beauty alone is stressed. It is
when she smites Holofernes :

> ' Slōh þā wundenlocc
> þone fēondsceaþan   fāgum mēce
> hete þoncolne...   ',

With a fine appreciation of dramatic contrast, the poet emphasises a characteristically feminine feature while he shews the
woman performing a peculiary virile action.

The heroic activity of the epic commonly implies the assertion
of individuality — as in Bēowulf, or in the heroes of Homer. In
Judith we find this activity made powerful by the surrender of
the personal, individual will to the will of God. It becomes in
this way superhuman ; the courage derived from religious conviction
plays the rôle of the legendary supernatural strength attributed
to Bēowulf and other heroes. Thus there is real fusion of content
and treatment between the old heroic Germanic epic and the Hebraic
religious narrative. The supreme will of God replaces the bleak

Wyrd of *Bēowulf* — though the idea of the latter, the Germanic belief in doom, still persists and finds occasional expression :

> '   hīe þæt fæge þāegon
> rōfe rondwīggende, þēah þæs se rīca ne wēnde... '.

But even this idea has become inextricably related to the conception of an omniscient God — the God to whom Judith addresses her prayer full of lyric beauty and compressed dramatic force :

> ' Ic þē frymþa God,   and frōfre Gāēst,
> Bearn Alwaldan   biddan wylle
> miltse þīnre   mē þearfendra,
> þrȳnesse þrymm.   þearle ys mē nū þā
> heorte onhāēted   and hige gēomor,
> swyþe mid sorgum gedrēfed ;   forgif mē, swegles Ealdor,
> sigor and sōþne gelēafan,   þæt ic mid þȳs sweorde mōte
> gehēawan þysne morþres bryttan ; geunne mē mīnra gesynta,
> þearlmōd þēoden gumena :   nahte ic þīnre nāēfre
> miltse þon māran þearfe :   gewrec nū, mihtig Dryhten,
> torhtmōd tīres brytta,   þæt mē ys þus torne on mōde'
> hāte on hreþre mīnum. '

Her act is one of heroism *and* vengeance, though the combination of motives is only indicated. The conventional religious moral follows — that the Lord helped her as He does all who turn to Him in faith. The response is immediate — 'þā wearþ hyre rūme on mōde' — and motivises the decisive act which follows.

The poet's main interest is in the figure of the heroine. This is an epic trait : the characters are grouped round a central personage. And although she is not drawn with any wealth of detail — the stereotyped epithets indeed prevent this — she is obviously the poet's chief concern. He troubles very little about Holofernes, and not at all about any minor characters. The epic method is in this the very reverse of the dramatic. What he does say of Holofernes, however, gives a graphic picture with a few broad strokes :

> ' hlōh and hlȳdde,   hlynede and dynede,
> þæt mihten fīra bearn   feorran gehȳran,
> hū se stīþmōda   styrmde and gylede,
> mōdig and medugāl   manode geneahhe
> bencsittende   þæt hī gebāērdon wel '.

It is significant that this is a portrait of Holofernes at the banquet, which, like the battle-scenes, was a theme congenial to the poet. He expands with native touches the more moderate picture of the Vulgate : 'Et iucundus factus est Holofernes ad eam, bibitque vinum multum nimis, quantum nunquam biberat in vita sua' (XII, 20). Otheiwise, Holofernes is described by epithets, varying from 'se bealofulla, wigena baldor' to 'þone hǽeþenan hund', according to the situation. Throughout we find the poet adapting the characters to native conditions ; Holofernes is no inaccessible Oriental despot, but a 'winedryhten', a 'sinces brytta' — in fact an Anglo-Saxon warrior chief, noted for conviviality and liberality. These epithets sound more genuine that the 'heathen dog' which we find when the poet remembers his chief theme and leaves the pleasant side-track of the Germanic feast.   He is equally at home in the descriptions of battle ; and the characteristic passage on the birds of prey : —

'
wulf in walde,	þæs se hlanca gefeah
wælgīfre fugel :	and se wanna hręfn,
þæt him þā þēodguman	wiston bēgen
fylle on fāēgum ;	þohton tilian
earn āētes georn,	ac him flēah on lāst
salowigpāda	ūrigfeþera,
hyrnednebba '.	sang hildelēoþ,

has the ring of Northern epic poetry.   It recalls similar lines in the Finnsburh fragment :

| ' Hwearf flacra hrāēw | hræfen, wandrode |
| sweart ond sealo-brūn '. | |

Those passages which express the spirit of the Germanic epic are of course additions and expansions of the original Vulgate narrative.   In chapter XV (6,7) of the Book of Judith we find the hint skilfully expanded by the poet into the description of the battle with the Assyrians.   This is the most notable addition to the account ; a less extensive one is the lament for Holofernes, in the elegiac tone characteristic of similar passages in *Bēowulf* :

' Hēr ys geswutelod	ūre sylfra forwyrd
tōweard getācnod,	þæt þære tīde ys
[nū] mid nīþum	nēah geþrungen,
þe wē sculon	losian somod,
æt sæcce forweorþan :	hēr līþ sweorde gehēawen,
behēafdod healdend ūre '.	

One or two minor deviations are of some interest. The plunder in the Vulgate consists of cattle and similar booty ; in the poem it is helmets, gold-adorned byrnies, which are laid at Judith's feet, as at those of a Saxon king. Similar adaptation of the story to the poet's own time is visible in the fact that Judith is not present at the feast of Holofernes — a definite alteration of the Apocryphal narrative, and characteristic for the domestic customs of the age. In the Vulgate account, Judith asks leave to go every night and morning outside the camp to pray (XIII, 12). At the point in the poem where this detail would naturally be mentioned — viz. when Judith and her maid escape from the camp to Bethulia — no reference is made to any arrangement that would give them free egress, and no explanation of their freedom is given. This, however, together with the fact there is no mention in the poem of a conclusion to the Achior episode (v. XIII, 27 and XIV, 6 of the Book of Judith) may be due to the fragmentary condition of the poem as we have it. But they may also be due to a dramatic concentration of the material ; and in this connection may be noted the condensation of Judith's long hymn of thanksgiving and praise (Book of Judith XIV) into a few lines of narrative proportionate to, and recalling, the opening lines of the fragment. There is no trailing epilogue ; the English poet had the gift of concise and vivid narrative in no less degree than that of epic breadth.

The Old English Judith is composed in the style of the poet who sang in the mead-hall of kings and nobles. In the so-called 'ältere Judith' — the earlier of the two Middle High German poems in the twelfth century Vorau MS. dealing with the theme — we hear the rougher notes of his successor, the 'Spielmann', or wandering singer of the eleventh century. The contrast is great. Here there is no epic breadth, no trace of epic convention ; the heroic tale becomes a popular ballad. And the ballad form seems to suit the story equally well. This is perhaps an indication of one of the main qualities of the subject — a quality still more strikingly manifested later in some of the dramatic treatments.

The writer was not interested in the connotations of the tale. There is hardly any indication that the war between Holofernes and the Jews is a war of religion, a battle for life or death. As in all ballad poetry, the interest is concentrated on the individuals, who appear, and act, against a background of circum-

stance that is taken for granted.   Holofernes is introduced as a
'herzog'

> ' der streit widir goti gerni :
> er hîz dî alliri wirsistin man
> sînin siti lernan...
> daz was dir argisti lîb :
> sît slûg in Judith ein wîb ' [1].

For Judith also the poet has a formula :

> '   ...dû gûti Judithi
> dû zi goti wol digiti : '

but it is a phrase, like any other ballad phrase, such as 'bold
Robin Hood' or the 'mirk midnight' ; it has not the weight of
meaning borne by the eipithets applied to Judith in the Old
English epic.   The phrases seize nevertheless a salient point of
character : e. g.

> '   ...Oloferni
> dî burc habit er gerni '

recalls at once the primary aim of Holofernes as a ballad antagonist.
   The rapid development of the duel between the two individuals
thus summarily placed in opposition to each other forms the content
of the poem.   Essentials only are related in concise narrative or
dialogue.   No superfluous details complicate the direct progress
of the action ; but neither is there room for any real description of
things or people.   It is even impossible, on occasion, to explain
the sequence of events or the way in which they occur.   Holofernes
marvels at the resistance of the citizens — and one would imagine
him to be speaking in his camp ; but immediately the 'burcgraf'
answers — apparently from within the city.   One of the citizens
takes up the argument, and Judith, hitherto only mentioned as
the future slayer of Holofernes, enters into the narrative, adorns
herself and goes out among the heathen.   These things do not
matter in the ballad.   No one wishes to explain how the Wife of

---

1. Quotations are taken from the convenient reprint in A. Waag : *Kleinere Gedichte des XI. u. XII. Jahrhunderts* (v. Bibliographical Survey N⁰ 4) where the poem
appears in the form now generally accepted as original.   For a discussion of the
problems of MS. authority and interpolations v. references given in Bibliographical
Survey.

Usher's Well received the news of her three sons, or how Sir Patrick Spens boarded the ship to Norway. The true ballad style provides a succession of effective moments ; each decisive step in the action is illuminated by a searchlight. The 'ältere Judith' is thus an interesting example of the art of the wandering singer ; indeed, Ehrismann goes so far as to call it 'ein Muster für den Stil eines epischen Volkslieds aus der mhd. Frühzeit ;...... *das einzige echte geistliche Spielmannslied*' [1].

It is indeed of great interest to find the biblical material moulded into this essentially popular form ; and the method of the Spielmann deserves note. Just as the English epic poet transformed the Eastern despot into a Germanic warrior-king, so the German singer changes the Oriental atmosphere into that of mediaeval Germany. Bathania (the name substituted for the Apocryphal Bethulia, possibly from the poet's recollection of the more familiar city in the New Testament [2]) is a 'burc', its governor a 'burcgravi', its chief priest 'biscof Bebilin', The formula 'in dirri burc dingi swer sō dir welli' recalls the terms of feudal lordship ; the biblical siege of twenty days is expanded into the ballad-like 'mēr danni ein jār' and the number of days asked for as a truce or 'vrist' is reduced from five to the favourite ballad number — three.

The most interesting point of comparison, however, is in the character of the ballad heroine. The Judith of the Spielmann, slightly sketched though she be, is obviously a very different person from her biblical prototype, or indeed from the Judith of the Old English epic poem. She is of course beautiful, and conscious of her beauty :

> ' sû was diz allir schônis wîb.
> sû zîrte woli den ir lîb. '

Holofernes, on beholding her, calls her 'ein wîb lussam', 'das schôni wîb'. It is worth noting that Holofernes is the first to see her approach. There is no machinery of guards and interviews in the simplified ballad version, for the poet's aim is to convey,

---

1. *Geschichte der deutschen Literatur bis zum Ausgang des Mittelalters.* 2ter Teil, 1. München, 1922, p. 104.

2. Cp. the title of Samuel Hebel's play. (Bibliographical Survey Nº 21) v. also A. Wallner in P. B. B. vol. XLIII. p. 190 (note 1), where a parallel instance in Lamprecht is cited (cp. Lamprechts *Alexander* ed. K. Kinzel, Halle 1884 (p. 82). (Vorauer) v. 649).

as directly as possible, the deep impression made on her antagonist·
Characteristic of the ballad manner is the couplet which follows :

> ' Dî kamerâri daz gihôrtin
> wī schîri si dar kêrtin !'

Judith immediately takes the initiative in the action. It is to
be supposed that she has heard the exclamation of Holofernes that
he will die if he does not obtain her ; for she addresses him at once :

> ' nu daz alsô wesin sol,
> daz dû, kuninc, mich zi wîbi nemin solt ' —

and suggests to him the preparation for the usual feast of the
'brûtlouft' — a Germanic custom. Germanic also is the legend
of overcoming an adversary by making him incapable at a
banquet [1], and it is especially noteworthy therefore that the feast
is suggested by Judith and not by Holofernes. She also takes an
active part in it [2] :

> ' dô schancti dû gûti Judithi
> dû zi goti weli digiti,
> sû undi iri wîb Âvi,
> dî schanctin wol zi wâri,
> der zenti [3] saz ûffin der banc,
> der hetti din wîn an dir hant.
> dô dranc Holoferni,
> dî burc dî habit er gerni :
> durch des wîbis klûgi
> er wart des wînis mûdi. '

The poem breaks off after the response of the angel to Judith's
prayer. Her last recorded act ist he stealing of Holofernes' weapon.
After she has done this, she prays to God for her people — 'dis
armin giloubigin' ; an angel appears and gives her detailed
instructions, which take the place of any personal resolve.

A much longer and less interesting version of the Judith theme
is also to be found in the Vorau MS. The 'jüngere Judith', as it
is usually called, is a didactic poem, an elaborate paraphrase of the

---

1. Ehrismann quotes an interesting parallel in the O. Norse *Atlakvipa*. *op. cit.*
p. 105, note 1.

2. Cp. K. Weinhold : *Deutsche Frauen in dem Mittelalter*, 3te Auflage, Wien, 1897.
vol. II, p. 123.

3. Zenti = ezzenti ? v. A. Wallner, *art. cit.* p. 192.

biblical story, punctuated by somewhat obvious moralisings. Throughout the centuries this kind of treatment of the subject is frequent ; the uninspired versification of a biblical theme was not beyond the powers of the most mediocre practitioner, and there was obviously credit to be gained from the popularisation of any portion of the Scriptures.   In kind, therefore, the 'jüngere Judith' of the Vorau MS. may be compared with the treatment of the story in the Weltchronik of Heinrich von München (Chronological Survey No. 7), the *Historie of Judith in the forme of a poem* by Du Bartas (No. 23), the 'Meisterlied' of 1607 (No 30), the narrative poem *Von Judith der Grossmüthigen* (No. 47), the romance of 1849 and the short narrative poem of 1854 (Nos. 86 and 87). There is little interest of treatment in any of these versions, precisely because they are didactic in aim and photographic in method, but the 'jüngere Judith' may perhaps be considered as an example of the type.

> ' Daz ne wirt iuch niuht verdaget,
> iz ne werde iu allez gesaget ' ;

the poet opens his tale with these words, and he faithfully fulfils his promise. He also outlines his programme in the didactic manner :

> ' Also an disem liede ist vil gut schin,
> wie er siu beschirmte, mit einem bloden wibelin,
> unde mit welcher schande
> Er Nabuchodonosors her sande wider ze lande '.

Some idea of the lack of interest in the poem may be derived from the description of Holofernes, which follows on a long account of the armies and lands of Nabuchodonosor :

> ' der was geheizen Holofernes.
> der chunich gedaht im des ;
> daz in dem lande ne waere
> ein man so richer noch so herer.
> ...Er was ein helt vil frumich,
> Er wart sa des hers chunich.
> ...Er was ein helt erlich. '

This detached presentation does not even seem due to any idea of dramatic impartiality in the poet, for he later expresses as great satisfaction at the fall of Holofernes as if he had really pourtrayed him as a tyrant. Two lines, in the style of popular poetry, give a more vivid impression of Holofernes than all the rest of the description of his character ; he has been ordered to conquer the rebellious lands, and the poet adds, obviously with an echo of ballad poetry :

> ' Also er die rede vernam,
> Hei wie schiere er uf chom. '

Judith is

> ' ein vil edel wip,
> scône was der ir lip. '

The poet is very mindful of Judith's piety ; he lays great stress on her grief and fasting during her widowhood, possibly in order to counterbalance the detailed description of her apparel when she goes to conquer Holofernes. For he is careful to add to this description an explanation recalling the warnings of the preacher in the Old English *Homily against Excess of Apparel* :

> ' wandiz neur nicht von iunchlicher ubermut,
> niewan von ir tugeden vil gut. '

The effect of her beauty on Holofernes is described in the stereotyped phrase of the mediaeval love-song :

> ' do begunde er sa brinnen
> nach ir edelen minnen '.

Throughout the poem Judith is a passive heroine ; in this she forms a complete contrast to the figure in the older Middle High German poem. The account of the actual slaying of Holofernes is very brief :

> ' Da nam si sin spert (=swert)·[uz der scheide ?]
> dem herren al ce leide,
> ich sage iu daz ceware,
> si vie in bi dem hare,
> unde sluch im also geburche
> daz hobet von dem buche. '

The song of praise is not reproduced ; the poet only alludes to it, and completes Judith's story by telling how

> ' die vrôwe was iemer mere ane man '

and was buried in honour beside Manasses [1].

---

1. For a full discussion of the sources of the poem v. the dissertation of J. Pirig referred to in the Bibliographical Survey (No. 5).

This poem is typical of the didactic treatments of the subject.
German traits and customs are introduced in such phrases as
'vursten, herzogen unde graven', 'Ozias der biscolf', 'Joachim der
erzebiscolf', 'die Holofernes helde', and in the lists of weapons and
of musical instruments, which are thoroughly nationalised. But
in spite of these efforts to make the story more vivid, the poem is
lifeless and monotonous. Its conception and execution are prosaic;
there is nothing of the inspiration of the Old English epic, or the
sheer delight in story of the earlier Middle High German ballad.
The dramatic moments of the tale are disregarded ; the descriptions
are tame accumulations of detail. The object of the writer was
utilitarian, and the poem affords convincing proof of it. Its
interest lies, as does that of the other examples of didactic treatment,
in the attempt to satisfy the secular taste of a knightly audience
by a biblical story which lent itself to the inculcation of the
appropriate moral.

Of a slightly different kind are the poetical versions of the Book
of Judith which have as their avowed object the application of the
story to contemporary historical, literary, and æsthetic conditions.
Such versions still belong to the category of didactic poetry, but
their aim is specific as well as general ; and they are interesting
as shewing one of the main reasons why treatments of the story
continued. The subject is dealt with in this way in the poetry of
the Teutonic order, which colonised East Prussia. Members of the
Order delighted in likening themselves and their history to biblical
personages and events; Joachim's *Kronike von Pruzinlant* contains
three references to Judith in this connection [1], and a 13th century
poem preserved in one MS. of the late 14th or early 15th century
treats the subject at length [2]. The writer is careful to give the
exact date of his poem [3]. From an envoy to a friend, in which he
sends the poem for criticism, from his own statement 'ich bin iunc',
from the emphasis which he lays throughout on his inability to do

---

1. *Di Kronike von Pruzinlant des Nicolaus von Jeroschin,* herausgeg. v. E.
Strehlke, in Hirsch : *Scriptores Rerum Prussicarum* vol. I (pp. 291 ff.) Leipzig, 1861.
(ll. 2304 ff. 2796 ff. & 3320 ff.)

2. For a discussion of the connection of this poem with the Teutonic Order v. M.
Hering's dissertation cited in Bibliographical Survey under No. 6.

3. For its date v. K. Helm in P. B. B. vol. XLIII. pp. 163-168, where the con-
jecture of " ein und zibenzic " for " ein und zwenzic " allows the more likely date
of 1304 to be substituted for 1254, which is unduly early for a poem of the Teutonic
Order. (v. also Anz. f. d. A. vol. LXII. p. 149).

justice to his task, and from the somewhat clumsy construction of
the poem, it is legitimate to conclude that Judith was his first
work.

He gives us not only the actual narrative, but a prologue and
epilogue, and a 'mystic-allegorical' portion which explains the true
meaning of the story He proposes to elaborate the biblical
account ;

> ' uf daz ez dir bequeme
> werde, so wil ich dar in
> noch mê tihtende sin
> dan in dem buche ist geschriben. '

He amplifies each event, not always artistically, he adds
'allegorical' explanations such as

> ' Egyptus vil gewisse
> bedutet vinsternisse ',

and he gives explanations of the proper names, borrowed from
Hieronymus' *De nominis Hebraicis*.   This is typical of the allegorical
treatments of the subject ; to add and to explain are methods
characteristic of the didactic writer pursuing a definite moral aim.
Similar devices are to be found in Henry Lok's 'Spiritual Sonnet',
where Bethulia is the 'bower of flesh', besieged by Holofernes
(who incarnates the power of sin) and rescued by faith's true
fountaine in a 'female couragde heart'. [1]   Again, in the *Meysterlied
von der Gottsförchtigen Frawen Judith* of 1607, a moral epilogue
serves a similar purpose.   Here four complicated stanzas suffice
for the story, dramatically condensed, and for the epilogue ; in the
latter we are told that Holofernes is the devil, who has besieged
us on all sides, through the eternal curse which lies upon us.   But
Christ delivers us from him ; and His death is 'das heilsame
Schwerdt' which Judith uses.

Closely connected with the didactic and allegorical tendencies
is the use of the Judith story as an illustration of the law of Nemesis.
The sudden fall of man from power to impotence was the mediaeval
definition of tragedy ; and of this Holofernes provided an excellent
example.   In Heinrich von Meissen des Frauenlobes 'Sprüche',
the story is outlined and stress is laid on this point :

---

1. v. Henry Lok : *Sundry Christian Passions* Pt. I, sonnet LXXXIII.   (Chronological Survey No. 27).

> Dô Olofern mit grimme
> sô krefticlîche erwelde,
> ein hôhez kûnecrîche
> jô er betwanc mit strîte,
> daz ez im zinses pflac.
> Waz half sîn breitiu menge ?
> ein wîp in doch erquelte,
> kein helt kam im ze troste :
> daz kam von gotes stâte,
> daz Judit in betrôch [1].

In the most considerable reference to the Judith story in the works of Chaucer [2], a similar moral is pointed. The title of the tale told by the Monk is 'De Oloferno' ; it shews at once the point of view, which is immediately further emphasised :

> ' Tragedie is to seyn a certeyn storie,
> As olde bokes maken us memorie,
> Of him that stood in greet prosperitie,
> And is y-fallen out of heigh degree
> Into miserie, and endeth wrecchedly '.

In the last of the three stanzas, the woman is contrasted with the tyrant :

> ' And yit, for al his pompe and al his might,
> Judith, a womman, as he lay upright,
> Sleping, his heed of smoot... '.

Chaucer seems to have been interested in the story of Judith. There are three other references to it in his works, besides the one already noted. In one (Man of Lawes Tale, ll.939 ff.)she is cited as an eminent example of weakness armed by God against strength. In this she is likened to the heroine Custance :

> ' Who yaf Judith corage or hardinesse
> To sleen him, Olofernus, in his tente,
> And to deliveren out of wrecchednesse
> The peple of God ? '

In the Marchantes Tale (ll.1365 ff.) stress is laid on her 'wys conseil' :

> ' By wys conseil she goddes peple kepte,
> And slow him, Olofernus, whyl he slepte. '

---

1. v. Chronological Survey No. 8.
2. v. Chronological Survey No. 8 for complete references.

is also one of an interminable list of illustrations adduced
udence in the Tale of Meliboeus to prove the fact that women
had 'good conseil' — a statement which Meliboeus has rashly
ied, thus drawing down upon his head a lengthy dissertation
most of the famous women of the Bible.

It is evident that the story was and remained popular, and that
various moral conclusions could be drawn from it. It seems
probable, moreover, that this latter reason may have accounted
for the ballad treatments of the tale, which are unfortunately lost,
but of whose existence there is clear evidence. Two entries in the
Stationers' Register of the 16th Century (1566-7 and 1588) record
the licensing of two ballads on 'Judith and Holofernes' to two
printers ; and a third version, obviously didactic, is cited by Hazlitt
as one of the *libri desiderati* (1565) [1].

The ballad of 1588 was licensed with two other didactic ballads
under the patronage of the Bishop of London — the first of them
being entitled 'A moste excellent new ballad Dyaloguewyse betwene
Christe and the soule of man', and the third 'A proper newe ballade
dyaloguewyse betwene Sinceritie and wilfull Ignorance' [2]. It is
plain that this version of the Judith story may be placed in the
category of popular tracts ; the ballads, printed often on single
sheets, hawked through the streets of London, and then scattered
to all parts of the country, catered for the public taste as does the
cheap fiction of today, and the element of adventure, combined
with the obvious moral of the tale, may well have contributed to
its inclusion in this class of literature. The applicability of the
story to contemporary conditions, noted already in the poetry of
the Teutonic Order, no doubt played a part in its widespread
popularity in the 16th century. This is certainly the case in many
of the dramatic versions which appeared in Germany and Austria.
In the *Judith* of Wolfgang Schmeltzl, for example, both prologue
and epilogue emphasise the dangers of Turkish attack, and exhort
the people of Vienna to take courage from the Scriptural story. [3]
Similarly, Sixt Birck sees in the narrative a topical moral. He
writes plays for young scholars which 'administrandae Reipublicae

---

1. v. Chronological Survey Nos. 22, 24, 20.

2. v. E. Arber : *Transcript of Stationers' Register* (quoted in Bibliographical
Survey Nos. 22 & 24) vol. II. Register B. 227.

3. v. the monograph on Schmeltzl by F. Spengler, quoted Bibl. Survey No. 12,
pp. 41-42.

aliquem imaginem prae se ferunt', and begins by addressing the 'junge Burgerschafft' and comparing the situation in the story with the contemporary troubles with the Turks [1].

Indeed, when we turn to a consideration of the dramas on the story of Judith, we find that while the tale is, as has been seen, a favourite subject for narrative poetry of various kinds, its popularity as a dramatic theme is much more remarkable. From the academic drama of Joachim Greff in 1536 — the first extant Germanic drama on the subject — to the latest versions of Sturge Moore, Georg Kaiser, Arnold Bennett and others in the twentieth century, a constant succession of plays testifies to its peculiar appeal to the dramatic sense. At first, no doubt, the story merely shared in the general popularity of biblical narratives as themes for academic drama ; later, however, it seems to have eclipsed the majority of them in importance. Luther, in his preface to Tobias, commends the dramatic qualities of the story : ,Denn Judith gibt eine gute, ernste, tapfere Tragödien ; so gibt Tobias eine feine, liebliche, gottselige Komödien'. [2] It is easy to realise the possibilities of the subject from a dramatic point of view. The fundamental antagonism of the two main characters — and here Holofernes comes into his own, in contrast to the epic and narrative versions — the fluctuation of interest from camp to camp and the variation of setting and atmosphere thus made possible, the rich opportunities for dramatic effect in the clash of the two characters and the rapid movement of the story, are all essentially dramatic qualities inherent in the material. Whereas the epic treatment primarily shews the heroism of the tale, and the didactic versions emphasise its moral of man's dependence on divine aid, the dramatic treatment of the subject lays supreme emphasis upon the essential conflict. But this dramatic virtue does not appear at first ; centuries pass before its possibilities are fully developed in the psychological drama of the 19th century. In the beginning, the dramatic and narrative versions strongly resemble one another. Hans Sachs treats the subject in both forms ; and only the technique and the dialogue differ slightly. Especially in the 16th century did these simple biblical plays find favour ; drama was emerging

---

1. v. infra. pp. 43 & 45.

2. Martin Luther : *Vermischte deutsche Schriften* ed. J. K. Irmischer ; vol. XI (Vorreden) (*Sämmtliche Werke* vol. LXIII. 4te Abtheilung.) Frankfurt a /M. u. Erlangen, 1854, p. 99.

from the early phase of Mystery and Miracle plays, but the Scriptural tradition was still strong, and in the stirring times of the Reformation such popular versions of biblical themes became useful vehicles of propaganda for both parties. The subject of Judith was a favourite one. With its moral of freedom from tyranny and the dependence of the weaker on the help of God, and with its implication of immediate revelation from on high, it served the Reformers excellently as a vehicle for propaganda against enemies of the faith, both within and without (as we have already seen, explicit references to the Turks, represented by Holofernes, are not wanting [1]). On the other hand, it shared the popularity of the stories of Esther, Mary Magdalen, Lazarus, and the Prodigal Son, as a theme for the Jesuit scholastic drama, as is evident from the large number of records in the annals of the various foundations of the Order. Many of the versions arose out of the need for instruction and practice in Latin (or, later, in the vernacular tongue) and in versification ; and doubtless the edification which was supposed to result from the handling of biblical material by the scholars helped to spread the custom of composing these dramas.

The close connection of the popular plays or ‚Volksschauspiele' with the Jesuit drama increased the natural preference for biblical subjects in the former ; and we find in fact several records of Judith plays, together with a specimen of later date which is accessible in print [2]. While the Jesuit influence thus lived on in the plays of the people, it also survived in the diversions of princes — viz. in the Opera or Singspiel. Originally a serious rival to the Jesuitenkomödie, this form of play in Germany soon shewed the influence of the latter ; while the later Jesuit dramas of the 18th century have much in common with the opera imported from Italy, the operatic play also shews a certain community of subject and decoration with the academic plays of the Order.

Thus it comes about that a very large number of records concerning the performance of Judith dramas is to be found from the 16th to the 18th century, as well as a number of plays actually preserved ; and each type of treatment shews some characteristic features.

The extant versions of the Reformers all reveal a primarily

---

1. Cp. Sixt. Birck : *Judith*. Drama comico-tragicum... Unde discitur, quomodo arma contra Turcam sint capienda. Augsburg 1540 (?).

2. v. Chronological Survey, No. 68.

pedagogic purpose.   In the drama of Joachim Greff, Judith shews the protection of God against Papal tyranny, and the epilogue consists of a long moral discourse on the meaning of the characters— Holofernes represents Pride, and Judith Faith.   The prevailing unbelief of the times evokes a protest from the dramatist :

> ' Doch steckt uns der unglaub so tieff im rachn,
> Das man stets mehr Holofernis find
> Denn die der Judith einlich sind. ' [1]

Rose, in his *Holofern* (1648) defines his position even more plainly.   His first object is to confirm his scholars in true Christian learning (i.e. Lutheran theology) ; his second, to give them practice in 'der reindeutschen Häupt=und Muttersprache', and to exercise them in rhetoric.   To this end he caused his pupils themselves to write the dialogues and soliloquies which make up his dramas. He calls the plays 'rhetorice disponieret', and the speeches are written in prose [2].

The avowed object of Sixt Birck's drama (Chronological Survey No 10) is more political : its title is of interest, for it shews how the subject could be adapted to the conditions of the time (and there is no doubt that this was one of the causes of its popularity) : ' Drama comico-tragicum.   Exemplum Reipublicae recte institutae.   Unde discitur quomodo arma contra Turcam sint capienda.' [3]   Emphasis is laid throughout Sixt Birck's drama on this political element in the narrative.   The Prologue (which appears in the early editions)

---

1. J. Greff : *Tragedia des Buchs Judith*. Wittemberg, 1536. Epilogus. (Chronological Survey N⁰ 9).

2. v. *Roses Geistliche Schauspiele* ed. H. Begemann, Berlin, 1913 pp. 5-7. (Chronological Survey N⁰ 38).

3. The title varies in different reprints.   The one quoted above appears in the edition published at Augsburg in 1540 (?) and in that published at Cologne in 1544 ; in the collected *Dramata Sacra* published by J. Oporinus at Basel in 1547, the phrase " Unde discitur... capienda " does not appear ; while in an edition of 1611 (Lavingae. i. e. Lauingen) it is replaced by " Specimen continens firmissimi civitatis praesidij" (In this edition the controversial " Prologus " is omitted).   It is worth noting that these differences roughly correspond to international affairs ; in 1539, war had broken out again between Austria and the Sublime Porte on the question of the Hungarian succession ; in 1541 and the following years Solyman himself was in command on the Danube, and until 1544, when Charles V and Ferdinand made overtures for peace, the general advantage was to the Turks.   In 1547 a truce was concluded for 5 years (including a yearly payment by Austria of 30.000 ducats).   In 1566 a new German war broke out ; but the year 1606 saw the conclusion of a peace by Treaty.   (v. Sir Edward S. Creasy : *History of the Ottoman Turks*.   London 1878. pp. 172 & 239).

gives the clue to this treatment.   It is a matter of common contro-
versy, he explains in the opening lines, whether military force should
be employed by Christians ('num fas sit arma Christiano sumere').
Wars differ in cause and justification : —

> ' Si belli causa quaeritur legittima
> Princeps certat de paruo territorio,
> Aut gentium ius est uiolatum... '.

Within the Christian world are many internecine wars : 'eo magis
lamentis et suspirijs Ploranda nobis daemonis uersutia'.   But

> ' Quid ergo Turca ?   Barbarossa barbarus ?
> Quid ipse Gallus [1]?   Quid Nebuc (b) adnezer est ?
> Ecquid Philistin ?   Quid Pharaon Aegyptius ?
> Quid Assyrius Holophernes hoc in dramate ? '

The matter is simple after all, in the 16th century.   There is
but one criterion for judgment :

> Si te iubet Dominus ferro decernere,
> Est auspicatum crede bellum... [2]

If war arises with the barbarous Turk, 'His machinis uincemus'.
Penitence and the recognition of sin, the amending of the lives of
Christians, will ensure the victory of their arms.   This is the moral
of the Judith story ; and we are led immediately to the 'Argumentum', while, in order that nothing may be left to chance, the
Epilogue demonstrates 'quae sit utilitas' — the familiar argument
in favour of drama :

> Neque enim mali ominis, ut multi garriunt,
> Huiusmodi ludi sunt, sed plenissimi
> Fructu bono, & documentis pertinentibus
> Uitae ad statum communis, nostro tempore

---

1. " Quid ipse Gallus " is deleted and a harmless phrase substituted in the
margin in the copy belonging to the Jesuit College in Munich (1544 edition Staatsbibliothek, München). v. infra, p. 66 (1).

2. The Epilogue to Sixt Birck's German play (Chronological Survey N° 11)
does not preach quite the same doctrine ; in it he says (perhaps with an even more
appropriate moral) ;

> Darinn mag auch ein fäler sein
> So man in einem guten schein
> Beschirmen will das vatterland
> Und nimpt trutz /neid uñ hass fürdhand'.

Potissimum, quo saeuit hostis impius,
Sititque nil, quam Christianum sanguinem,
Qui deuorauit orbis partes plurimas.

. . . .

Cum Turca trux incursionem factitat
In regna nostra, tum pio precamine
Et poenitentia expiemus crimina
Uitae prioris.   Hae sunt uerae machinae.
Licet quidem nobis pro chara patria
Pugnare, proque Christiano nomine : '

All this is a more obvious pointing of the moral than modern
taste approves, but its interest is somewhat apart from purely
dramatic considerations : it explains the popularity of the theme
among the Reformers of the 16th century and shews its application
to life.   It would be possible to argue that an even more modern
note is struck by Sixt Birck in the 'Prologus' [1]. Martin Böhme,
although in general dependent on Sixt Birck, does not echo his
political views.   The long prologue to *Vom Holoferne und der
Judith* ends with the words' : 'Auff gottes Lob man einig sicht
Und auff der Menschen Heil mans richt' [2].

Hans Sachs, in contrast to Sixt Birck, contents himself with
writing a 'comedi' (Chronological Survey N⁰ 14) without any very
definite aim beyond that of dramatising a biblical episode.   Most
of these versions, indeed, follow the Apocryphal narrative closely,
without much attempt at dramatic arrangement.   Hans Sachs
only condenses it in one or two particulars, such as the conciseness
of Achior's speech to Holofernes relating the history of the Jews,
and the omission of the scene where Achior is found, tied to a tree,
by the citizens of Bethulia. (Reference is made to this incident in
Act II, scene 2 — an unusual example of dramatic concentration).
The natural consequence of this close reproduction of the narrative

---

1. In the earlier German version, the Prologue is much shorter ; it is addressed
to " ein iunge Burgerschafft ", but deals first of all with the contrast between
" Tugend " and " Reichtum " ; later he instances Judith as an illustration of the
former and adds :

" Fraw Judith mag uns lernen wol
Wie man den Türcken schlagen sol...
...Ich wolt das inn meim Vatterland
Solch ehrlich Übung wurd an dhand ".

In the " Beschlussred " a definite moral is attached to Judith and her counsel.

2. *Tragicomoedia... vom Holoferne und der Judith.* Wittenberg 1618. (p. 6)
(Chronological Survey N⁰ 31).

is that in all the dramas there is a long exposition. In Greff's version, Judith does not appear until Act III, when she immediately delivers a long sermon to Ozias ; in the German drama of Sixt Birck she makes her entry in the 14th dialogue (corresponding to Act IV of his Latin version) ; Hans Sachs begins at the very beginning of the story with Nabuchodonosor's council of war and Judith appears in the last scene of the second Act ; in the *Tragicomoedia* of Martin Böhme she appears in the fourth scene of Act II ; and in the Latin drama of Cornelius Schonaeus the heroine first enters in Act IV, scene 2, after which all the real action takes place. Thus of action there is sometimes extraordinarily little ; in Greff's treatment, for example, (where Judith appears in Act III) the action ends with Act IV, and the fifth Act is merely in the nature of an epilogue of prayer and praise [1].)

A general characteristic of mediaeval drama which is noticeable in the plays of Judith is the disregard of change of scene and lapse of time. In Act IV, scene 6, of Greff's *Judith* there is no change of scene, although three sets of speakers carry on the dialogue in different places. Again, in the seventh scene of the same act, Judith kills Holofernes, returns to Bethulia and is greeted there with rejoicing in one and the same scene [2]. Sixt Birck also records in one scene (Act V, scene 1 of the Latin drama) Holophernes' message to Judith by Vagao, the delivery of the message and her reception of it, Vagao's return to his master, and the arrival of Judith in response to the summons sent her [3] ; while Hans Sachs makes no attempt to register change of place, combining for example in one act (Act II) the dialogue of Holofernes and Achior (in the Assyrian camp), the consultation of Carmi and Osias (in Bethulia) the conversation of Holoternes and Pagoa, another discussion between Carmi and Osias, and finally the address of Judith to these elders [4].

---

1. It is perhaps of interest, in this connection, to compare the inorganic nature of the last act of the English academic tragedy of *Gorboduc*.

2. Cf. *Tragoedia Mundi* II, 9, (Chronological Survey No 37) where Judith attends the banquet, kills Holofernes, returns and is greeted in Bethulia.

3. An exactly parallel development of the scene is to be found in *Tragoedia Mundi* II, 8.

4. It is interesting to note that a copy of Sixt Birck's Latin drama (1544) in the Staatsbibliothek, München, which apparently belonged to the Jesuit College there, contains, among other more important marginal corrections and additions, stage directions added in writing. (v. infra, p. 66, note 1).

Such stage directions as there are in Greff's play are in Latin (the language of instruction); they deal in the main with exits and entrances, but in Act V, scene 1 they give an account of a battle. Two of the directions are of considerable interest : 'Hic cantabitur classicum apud Israelitas' (I, 3), and 'Hic classicum cantabitur in castris Holofernis' (II, 2 and V, 1). Here evidently was a chorus of scholars singing an aria in classical lyric measures [1], the text of which was memorised and not inserted. Sixt Birck uses the chorus at intervals throughout his German drama, and introduces in section 3 a prayer in lyric stanzas, with the direction : 'Zu singen wie die Sapphica' [2]. His stage directions in the German version are in German ; moreover, they attempt, to a greater degree than Greff's, to describe the action which should accompany the dialogue — e. g. (in section 12) : ' Unnd weil der rhat sitzt, soll die gemeyn under einander weynen'. (It is noticeable throughout that Sixt Birck makes definite if crude attempts to convey the impression of the crowd as taking part in the action). The 'Ehrnhold' in the Prologue to the *Judith* of Hans Sachs announces the matter of the play in these words :

> Wie das Büchlein Judith erklert
> Nun hört wie das erzelet werdt
> Nach leng mit worten und geberdt'.

And in conformity with this dramatist's usual habit, the stage directions referring to the 'geberdt' are detailed : 'neigt sich' 'hebt die hend auff', 'weynet', and similar phrases frequently occur. Martin Böhme writes his stage directions (with one exception) in German, and describes in them the actions of the characters ; while Christian Rose eventually shews in the elaborate detail of his staging and scenic directions a trend similar to that of the Jesuit drama in its development towards the operatic genre [3]. Music,

---

1. Cp. the early editions of Sixt Birck's *Judith* Drama comico-tragicum (1540 (?) and 1544) where the chorus immediately following the Argumentum (and taken from Psalm XLVI) is accompanied by the direction : "Tricoli tristrophi, constans primo uersu Glyconico, Secundo Asclepiadaeo, Tertio Choriambico... " Similar directions are to be found for the chorus at the end of each act, and after the Epilogue the final chorus, " canticum Judith ", is " uersu Coriambico Asclepiadaeo, *ut illud Horatij* : Moecenas atauis etc. ".

2. Cp. the chorus in the Latin drama IV. 7 (Ps. LXX) " sub persona Bethuliae, uersu Sapphico ". (edd. of 1540 (?) and 1544).

3. v. infra p. 60. Rose. emphasises the importance of the inserted songs (ed. cit. pp. 5, 13) ; and the airs are printed at intervals throughout the play (ed. cit. pp. 112 ff. 228 ff. 264 ff. 310 ff. etc.)

both choral and instrumental, plays a large part in the action, while the pomp of the triumphal procession in Judith's honour at the end sufficiently indicates the kinship of this play to the general development of German drama during the 17th century.

Since the conception of Judith's character and mission is the main point of interest in the treatment of the story, it is incumbent on us to inquire how far these early dramatic versions mark an advance in comprehension or solution of the problems presented by the main figures of the tale ; and from this point of view it must be admitted that the majority lack any great interest. Perceptible advance is evident however in Sixt Birck's plays. Judith shews dignity and firmness of resolve ; she also has initiative and power as well as religious trust and the faculty of self-surrender. The clearest manifestation of her character is in her prayer (section 15 of the German drama), where she reveals her plan of making Holofernes fall in love with her, to his own destruction. Her deed is called, in terms of the highest praise, 'Ritterschaft', and she is 'theure Ritterin'. There is here some appreciation of the virility of her achievement — a suggestion borne out by the speech of the Elders concerning her in section 14 :

> Chambri : Die Fraw ist aller weissheyt vol.
> Charmi : Sie kan auch mächtig reden wol.
> Ozias : Ey, warumb ist sie nit ein man ?
> Chambri : Gott hat sie wöllen also han'.

That this is the deliberate conception of her nature is evident from the 'Vorrede', where the dramatist speaks in person :

> ' Darumb ich für ein fassnachtspyl
> Euch für die augen stellen wil
> Ein *redlich mannlich dapffer weib*
> Die hat gewaget iren leib
> Zu retten ir volck statt und land ' [1].

Holofernes is pictured as the proud despot, vowing vengeance on the tiny city : 'In dem.... *tobet* Holofernes mit disen worten :

> ' Sie müssen würcken wol die buss
> Keyn steyn beym andern bleiben muss
> Darzu in muter leib das kind
> Muss mercken das wir seien feind

---

[1]. This description gains in interest if we compare it with the problem which Hebbel finds in Judith's character. v. infra, pp. 96-97.

Keyns schonen weder iung noch alt
Es muss als brechen mit gewalt '.

But in contact with Judith he is gracious as well as credulous :

Darum du liebste zarte mein
Kum zu uns in mein zelt herein
Bsich unser schätz und unser gut
Erlustig darob deinen mut.
Die speiss gend ir von meinem tisch
Es sey dann Wildtprät oder Visch '.

In naive fashion he announces at nightfall that he is 'des weins
zu voll, Der Kopff ist mir worden toll' — but otherwise shews no
signs of undue pride or intoxication ; and altogether he is a harmless
kind of tyrant, whose fall is motivised by circumstance rather than
by character.

The minor characters especially shew Sixt Birck's greater
technical skill ; they are more human, even vivacious in speech
and action (v. for example section 6, where Tychophylax and the
trumpeter spar with one another). Abra is drawn with a few
slight strokes, yet clearly. She is timid but devoted, afraid of
Judith's apparent recklessness, but confident in the God of her
fathers :

' Mir zweifelt gentzlich nit an Gott...
...Das wir damitten under in
Als schäflin bei der wölfen schar
Die sie umbgeben hond umbhar
Erretten unsern keuschen leib. '

She shews a certain amount of spirit on occasion too. On their
approach to Holofernes, when Judith commands her to bow before
'dem Hertzog fein', she replies, in spite of her qualms :

' Ja fraw ich kan die hoffzucht wol
Ich weiss wie man sich neygen sol '.

The people are characterised as fickle and uncertain. Chambri
summarises their nature thus :

· Das volck hat allenthalb die art
Dass nit lang in der trübsal bharrt ' ;

and this is borne out by the immoderate character of both their
lamentations and their transports. Some skill is shewn in the

handling of such situations as the dialogues among the servants and the guards of Holofernes, the interplay between the two maidens of Bethulia who find the well outside the city blocked and grumble at the decision of the Elders to resist Holofernes, or the vivid scene where Vagao finds his chieftain dead. Similarly, Sixt Birck's arrangement of the material marks an advance on that of Greff. Although in the German version the orthodox divisions of act and scene are absent, the action is dramatic [1]. There is a fairly skilful avoidance of repetition in the Achior episode ; whereas in Greff's drama he tells his tale first to the two Bethulians who release him and then to the Elders in the city, in Sixt Birck's he relates it only to the Elders, including in this narrative the incident of his release by the Bethulian citizens. (It must be admitted however that this improvement is partly counterbalanced by the extreme length of Achior's tale when he does tell it). A similar device is employed when Achior asks Judith, on her return to Bethulia, how she has succeeded in killing Holofernes, and she is thus given an opportunity of telling the story of her deed, the actual performance of which has not been pourtrayed in the preceding scenes.

All this marks out Sixt Birck as the possessor of some skill in dramatic writing ; though there are also clumsy expedients, improbabilities and repetitions in his work. As has been seen, change of scene and lapse of time are frequently disregarded ; the council which takes place in Bethulia while Holofernes is apparently waiting at the walls consists of a succession of speeches, neither dramatic nor interesting, and there is considerable improbability in its duration if the Assyrian chieftain is really supposed to be awaiting the decision of the assembly. Nevertheless, Sixt Birck's German play of *Judith*, as a whole, is an interesting early dramatic treatment. The Latin version of this play is also interesting. In the 'Argumentum' the character of Judith is indicated, as well as the course of the action :

> ' Judith uirago mente praesentissima,
> Periculis in ipsis plena consili,
> Belli molem totam in se sponte suscipit '.

---

1. This absence is the only feature which Gottsched finds to note in Sixt Birck's drama : " Diese Tragödie ist in keine Handlungen und Auftritte abgetheilet " (*Nöthiger Vorrath zur Geschichte der deutschen dramatischen Dichtkunst* Leipzig, 1757-65, Theil II, p. 218). In the Latin version the usual division into acts and scenes is found, with considerable expansion of the earlier part (Acts I-III).

Although Judith does not appear till the opening scene of Act IV, the power of her personality is clearly shewn.   She reproaches the senators with fire, even if her speeches are too long :

> '   salus tamen magis me patriae,
> Deique honor mouet, quam quod mos publicus
> Iubet.   Decoro iam cedat necessitas. ' [1]

After her victory over Holofernes, the maidens conversing at the well glorify her achievement :

> Herois ast Judith uictrix fortis est :
> Haec sexui nostro peperit hanc gloriam' —

a statement which leads immediately to an interesting discussion on women [2].   Finally, in the Epilogue, the author sums up his conception of Judith's character :

> ' Judith est cordata, fortis & pia,
> Pudica, constans & praesentis consili,
> Mirabilis suae est amatrix patriae.
> Non hic uides, quod est fere in nostratibus
> Mulieribus, quibus tantum loquacitas
> Studio est, inepta & arrogans superbia.
> Uiros suos reddunt pleraeque uxorios.
> Sed haec uiris plerisque habet plus pectoris,
> En territos confirmat forti robore.
> Et consulem & patres regit prudentia
> Sua, & senatum errantem pulchre corrigit ' [3].

It is plain that the civic interest of the story, which mainly attracted Sixt Birck, greatly influenced his presentation of Judith's character ; his emphasis on the marvel of her achievement in public life is worthy of note.

One of the most noticeable features in the *Judith* of Hans Sachs

---

1. In the corresponding scene in the German play, Judith's speech is more biblical, and emphasises less the civic than the religious aspect of the situation.

2. A scene closely corresponding to this is in the German play, and equal emphasis is laid on Judith's " mannligkeyt ".

3. In the epilogue to the German play, Judith's virtues are more shortly recited :
> " Du weibsbild schaw den spiegel an
> Den du hie magst in Judith han
> Hertz /mut /und manheyt ist bey jr
> Es staht bey jr nit wie bei dir
> Dir ist nur wol mit klapperey
> Gott geb wos bätt und Gottsforcht sei... ".

is its title : 'ein geistliche Comedi mit 16 personen unnd fünff actus'. Tragedy, to Hans Sachs, involved the killing of his principal characters at the end of the play, while comedy was the term applied to dramas of very varying types, as long as the hero or heroine survived. Hence it is interesting to find *Judith* called a comedy ; for this shews that the dramatist still has the old conception (similar to that of the narrative poems) of Holofernes as a tyrant and a villain, whose death does not affect the character of the 'comedi'. Evidently, however, he feels some slight compunction at the thought of Holofernes, for he explains in the Prologue :

> ' und haben alhie fürgenommen
> zu halten ein geistlich comedi,
> doch schier vast gleich einer tragedi [1] '.

Judith herself is an uninteresting figure in this drama. Holofernes, on the other hand, shews a certain amount of initiative. It is he himself (and not one of his officers) who suggests the expedient of blocking the wells whence the Bethulians draw their water ; and in the opening scene he gains the favour of Nabuchodonosor by advising war, while Pagoa, 'der hoffmeister', counsels peace. An impression of the force and violence of his character is thus created at the very beginning.

Such small additions as Hans Sachs makes to his previous narrative treatment shew some sense of the dramatic situation. In Act III, scene 2, when Holofernes is in deep perplexity as to his course of action, Judith arrives, seemingly with an offer of assistance. He says :

> ' ...Weil ich vorher in diesem Krieg
> Mit verretrey erlangt all Sieg,
> Kein Jud wil umb gelt und ducaten
> Sein eigen vatterland verratten,
> Wie andre völcker haben than ' ; —

and at this moment a Hebrew woman is announced, who declares she is willing to betray her city for the price of safety. It is true that we already know (from the preceding scene) that Judith's

---

1. Cp. Sixt Birck's Latin *Judith* : " Drama comico-tragicum ". The use (or misuse) of the term Tragi-comoedia (comico-tragoedia) seems to have been derived from Plautus (Prologus ad Amphitruonem 59) v. A. Jundt : *Die dramatischen Aufführungen im Gymnasium zu Strassburg*. Programm d. protestantischen Gymnasiums Strassburg 1881. p, 6.

purpose is to deceive Holofernes ; nevertheless the episode is an effective one.   A more striking instance of dramatic irony is in Act IV, scene 1, where Pagoa warns the guards to be more careful than usual, since the watch is incapable of action — an unusually indirect means of making known the drunkenness at Holofernes' banquet ; this ominous warning is succeeded in Act V, scene 1, by a speech of one of the guards concerning the night's revelry, in which the words occur :

> ' Wenns der feindt innen worden wer
> Er het uns wol ein abbruch than '.

Meanwhile we know that the greatest 'abbruch' of all has been accomplished by a woman's hand inside the camp.

In its main outlines, Martin Böhme's *Tragicomoedia Vom Holoferne und der Judith* agrees with Sixt Birck's treatment ; but the play lacks the dramatic interest of the earlier version.   The long speeches in which the generals of Holofernes characterise themselves as vainglorious flatterers (I, 1, and I, 4), the inordinate length of Achior's narrative, the wordy descriptions of the distress in Bethulia (II, 5, IV, 2), the detailed picture of the camp followers and the wedding of the 'Landsknecht' 'nach Kriegsleut art' (though this is of interest from other points of view) and finally the whole lengthy fifth act, combine to produce an impression of undramatic discursiveness, which is not redeemed — as it is in Sixt Birck's play — by some skill in characterisation.   The moralising speeches are uninteresting ; and even the scene where Bagoa discovers Holofernes dead has little dramatic effect.   Holofernes is quite a gentle tyrant and hardly seems to deserve his fate : he rebukes his generals as they strive to glorify themselves :

> Die that rhümt sich / und nicht der Mundt /
> Die Tugend macht sich selber kundt /   (I, 1).

and to Judith he says :

> Ich bin ein Mann / wie sonst ein Mann /
> Ein jeder mit mir reden kan.   (III, 5).

He is not impervious to the opinions of others, for he thus explains to Bagoa his summons of Judith to a banquet :

> Denn diss wer uns ein grosse schandt /
> Ich hett den spot in gantzen Landt /

> Das so ein wunder schön Person /
> Solt kommen ohne Lieb davon /
> Und solt mich äffen als ein Thorn /
> Man meint ich het mein Witz verlorn [1].   (III, 6).

Emphasis is repeatedly laid, however, on the fact that Judith's honour, by divine assistance, remains untouched. (Prologue, p. 5, IV, 3, and V, 4).   She ascribes all praise to God :

> Der Rhum ich gar nicht mir zu schreib /
> Ich bin ein schwach und furchtsam Weib.   (V, 2).

The contrast between her weak womanhood and Holofernes' might is frequently drawn :

> Weil doch durch Gott der Weiber rhat /
> Gar offt viel guts geschaffet hat.   (I, 4).

and in Judith's prayer (III, 3) :

> So wird man preisen deine Macht /
> Das ihn Weibs Hand hat umbgebracht /.

The symbolical meaning of this contrast is stated in the Epilogue :

> Der Holofernes GOTTES Feindt /
> Die Kyrch zu stürtzen wahr gemeint /
> ...Den stürtzt GOtt leicht durch Weibes Handt /
> Das er verderbt mit spot und schandt.
> So hat die Kyrch in dieser Welt /
> Zum Feind gar manchen kühnen Helt /
> Den kan GOtt bald zu Boden legn.

The last lines are undoubtedly applicable to contemporary conditions. Indeed, the most interesting parts of the play are those which obviously reflect these, together with the personal experience of the author, though from the point of view of dramatic structure such scenes as II, 5 and III, 7 are disproportionately long. But the descriptions of ravaged lands (I, 1), the state of hunger in Bethulia (II, 5), the accounts of greed and meanness among the people during times of privation (V, 3), and above all, the more vivid scene of the 'wedding' of the Landsknecht (III, 7) justify themselves by a quality of observation which is lacking

---

1. Cp. Book of Judith, ch. XII, 12.

in the presentation of the more important characters. A minor point of interest is Böhme's use of the premonitory dream in Act III, scene 4, where one of Holofernes' soldiers describes the vision he has had of a lamb overcoming a lion. His tale is overheard by Judith, who is encouraged and cheered thereby [1].

In the scene of Holofernes' death (IV, 1), the dramatist uses the favourite stage device of the curtain. Judith draws it apart at the beginning of the scene, and prays in the open space. Then she draws it together, and prays aloud inside the tent, while a sound is heard as of a stroke falling. Abra remains outside; her comments and prayer fill the interval until Judith draws the curtain aside, and 'bringt ein sonderlich dozu zugerichtes Heupt herfür / welches Holoferni ähnlich sihet / gibts der Magd in Sack zustechen / sie mus auch die Decken von Bette mitnehmen...' [2]

A final four-part song of praise concludes the drama and leads to the Epilogue ; in this Böhme foreshadows the musical developments in Rose's *Holofern* [3].

Rose's *Holofern* offers comparatively little that is interesting. in characterisation and dramatic method, for it was, as has been seen, primarily a compilation [4]. Moreover, Rose borrowed from other authors in the parts of the play not composed by his scholars ; he transcribed the songs and choruses in verse from Tscherning's expansion of Opitz's opera *Judith*, and Acts IV and V, with the exception of the end, were practically taken over from Tscherning and Opitz [5]. Similarly, in the use of prose, in the insertion of a burlesque interlude and of musical decoration, he took as his model the *Perseus* of Johann Rist (1634). Indeed, instead of troubling to copy out Rist's interlude — totally unconnected with the subject and inserted merely to please the public taste — he goes

---

1. Rose in his *Holofern* uses the dream similarly (Des 4. Haupt = Satzes ander Theil. ed. cit. pp. 206-7), but Judith is not affected by it. The use may be compared in its effect with the symbolical dumb show of the Jesuit dramas. v. infra, pp. 62 ff.

2. Cp. the technical devices of the Jesuit dramas in this matter. v. infra p. 63.

3. v. supra p. 47 (note 3).

4. v. supra, p. 43.

5. v. infra, p. 80. Rose acknowledges Opitz and not Tscherning as his source (Kleine Erinnerung an den Leser, *Holofern*, Hamburg, 1648, p. 12) ; but from a comparison of Acts I and II with the latter's version it seems clear that a copy of Opitz's successor was in his hands. While Opitz has only 8 characters and Tscherning 30, Rose increases the number to 80 (including the persons in the " Zwischenspiel"). v. *Roses Geistliche Schauspiele* ed. H. Begemann, Berlin, 1913. Introduction, pp. 43-45.

so far as to refer actors and readers to Rist's drama, where, he says, they will find the text[1]. The only part of the play which shews any original talent is that containing the natural and unaffected dialogues of the soldiers [2]. Here the personal experience of Rose and his scholars enabled them to write realistically, and, as in Tscherning's version, it is where the story contains incidents similar to those of the Thirty Years' War that the language becomes vivid and the pictures convincing. Holofernes (significantly, his name is the title of the play), is represented as the type of 17th century military tyrant known only too well between 1618 and 1648, and Rose has no ethical misgivings as to Judith's action in deceiving him.

While the Protestants thus used the Judith theme as one of the subjects of academic drama, a much more extensive development of it is to be found in the Jesuit 'Schulkomödie' [3]. These scholastic dramas aimed at the representation of a religious or ethical truth, for the benefit of both scholars and spectators. The play thus fulfilled the function of a sermon, and at the same time accustomed the scholars to ease of speech and movement in public and gave them practice in elocution. Moreover, the performance gave parents and patrons a picture of the school activities, and afforded an opportunity of expressing gratitude to founders and benefactors of the various Colleges.

In the rules of instruction of the Order, regulations as to the acting of plays are laid down [4]. The subjects of tragedies and comedies must be sacred ; the plays must be acted seldom, and only in Latin. The Interludes must not be unseemly, and there must be no women's rôles. (A dispensation for this last rule was sometimes given, as for instance in 1603, in the Oberdeutsche Ordensprovinz, on condition that the introduction of such rôles be rare, and that the persons represented be 'graves et modestae' [5]). The teacher may give his

1. *Holofern*, ed. cit. pp. 160, 200.

2. e. g. Des 2. Haupt = Satzes 5ter Theil. (ed. cit. pp. 144 ff), Des 4. Haupt = Satzes ander Theil. (ed. cit. pp. 205 ff.) or Des 4. Haupt = Satzes 7ter Theil (ed. cit. pp. 262 ff).

3. The first " Jesuitenkomödie " (the name " Komödie " was applied to all genres) was performed in Vienna in 1555. (v. Bernhard Duhr, S. J. *Geschichte der Jesuiten in den Ländern deutscher Zunge*. Freiburg i /Brg. 1907. vol. I, p. 331).

4. *Ratio Studiorum et Institutiones scholasticae Societatis Jesu* von G. M. Pachtler (in *Monumenta Germaniae Paedagogica* vol. V) Tomus II, ann. 1588, 1599, 1832) Berlin 1887, pp. 272-3 and 412-413.

5. *Ratio Studiorum, ed. cit.* Tomus II, p. 488.

pupils short scenes to work out, and may have the best one performed in the school, without staging, the rôles being taken by the scholars.

Gradually, however, these rules became more elastic, and were frequently evaded. The order concerning staging, for example, was modified by a 'nisi necesse sit' ; and the question of expense was solved by the patrons of the Order, who provided scenery, stage effects and costumes. The rule concerning the use of Latin remained longest in force, but in 1768 the Jesuits were ordered to act comedies in German, for the better instruction of their scholars in the mother tongue.

The plays themselves were for the most part not printed — possibly because they were meant to be an exercise of memory as well as of elocution, or because the pupils were expected to extemporise at the performance, after a certain amount of rehearsal. Printed 'programmes' or 'periochae' then gave the necessary information to the spectators — the title, the incidents of the story, the course of the acts and scenes, the lists of dramatis personae and the names of the actors. Hundreds of these programmes, even, must be irrecoverable ; originally they must have been printed in large numbers, but usually by now each one preserved of a particular play is a unique specimen [1]. Search in the annals of the Order yields abundant records of dramas on the subject of Judith; in Ingolstadt, Vienna, Luzern, Engelberg, Einsiedeln, Graz, Hildesheim, Landshut, München, Augsburg, Jülich, Heidelberg, Prag, Düsseldorf, performances are recorded, and sometimes dramas or periochae have been preserved ; while in Salzburg and Aachen records of 'Schuldramen' of a similar type to the Jesuit plays are found [2]. Sometimes, especially in those of later date, the German text of the Arias and choruses was given [3] ; others had outlines of the story both in Latin and in German [4].

1. Professor Karl Lechner (60. Programm des K. K. Staatsgymnasiums in Innsbruck 1908/9, Innsbruck, 1909, III, 13. *Dramatische Aufführungen*, p. 92) is of opinion that these " periochae " or scenarios were first printed in 1606. The average number printed in Innsbruck appears to have been 600 (v. *ibid.*, where a record of payment in 1655 to the printer M. Wagner for this number is quoted.) In Munich, however, the first " Programm " seems to have been printed earlier, in 1597. (v. J. Ehret : *Das Jesuitentheater zu Freiburg in der Schweiz*, 1ter Teil, Freiburg i /Brg. 1921, pp. 89 ff., where a full discussion of the various types of periochae is to be found).

2. v. Chron. Survey, passim.

3. v. *Judith*, 1763 (Aachen) Appendix B.

4. e. g. *Juditha* et *Holofernes* 1654 (Chron. Survey N° 41.) & *Victrix fiducia Bethuliae* (Appendix A).

Generally there was a prologue to the whole play, and sometimes a special prologue to each act ; and every act closed with a choric song (with or without instrumental accompaniment) to point the moral of the action [1].

The Prologue (Prolusio, or Praeludium, as it is variously called) usually represented, with symbolic figures akin to those of the Morality Play, the ethical teaching of the drama.   In the Prologue to a 17th century Latin drama on *Judith* (Engelberger Kloster-bibliothek, 1650) such characters as Uranostrategus, Judithophilus, as well as the Virgin, Jesulus, Esther, Jael, Ruth, Abigail, Narcissus and Adonis, take part in a debate on the strongest woman ; while the figures of Voluptas, Opulentia, Cupido, Castitas, Abstinentia, Timor Dei, etc. discuss Judith's piety in the opening scene [2].

The function of the chorus was to give the contents of the play in allegorical form ; thus it constituted a kind of 'Zwischenakt' or dramatised choric song.   The choruses in the drama of Nicolaus Avancinus (who entered the novitiate of the Jesuit Order in 1612 at Graz) illustrate this allegorical function : 'Chorus Timor Bethuliae' (in the first of whose three parts Greek mythological characters are introduced) closes Act I ; 'Chorus Dolor Bethuliae' Act II ; 'Chorus Spei', in which Spes comes down from heaven and converses with Bethulia, Act III ; and 'Chorus Gaudii' Act IV, where Fear and Grief are put to flight and Bethulia is lifted up into aether [3].   In the Latin *Judith* of 1650 (MS. Engelberger Klost-erbibliothek) short songs of angels (rhymed and unrhymed) end Acts I and II, while a symphony closes Acts III and IV., and in the middle of Act IV, when Judith accepts Holofernes' invitation to the banquet, the following indications are given : 'Musica e caelo', and 'classicum caelo venit'.   In the German drama *Tragoedia Mundi* (MS. Luzern, 1647) several arias occur, and the direction 'cantus' is frequent ; at the end of Act I, after the victory of Holofernes over Arphaxat, Apollo, Venus, Mercury and other Olympic deities sing a 'cantus classicus' and discuss the fate of Judea, while the second Act closes with a 'cantus' in elaborate metres sung by

---

1. Cp. Jakob Zeidler : *Studien und Beiträge zur Geschichte der Jesuitenkomödie und des Klosterdramas* (Theatergeschichtliche Forschungen, herausgeg. B. Litz-mann, vol. IV) Hamburg u. Leipzig 1891, pp. 86, 88, 90, 92.

2. Cp. the summaries of the Chorus at the end of each Act in *Victrix. fiducia Bethuliae* (Appendix A.)

3. Cp. also *Judith* 1763 (Periocha, Aachen, Appendix B.) where in the prologue Providence shews the significance of the action.

Flora, Clara, Bella, Hofnung etc. [1]. In the drama *Judithae de Holoferne triumphus* of 1720, (MS. Staatsbibliothek München) [2] the chorus at the end of each of the three parts (Bethulia Pressa, Bethulia Relevata, and Bethulia Liberata) celebrates a moral triumph in hymnlike chants with refrains.   These songs are assigned to 'genii', allegorical figures represented as satellites to Ambitio on the one hand and to the people of Israel on the other.   That at the end of Part I is headed 'Uirtus probatur non reprobatur aduersis' ; that at the end of Part II 'Spes confisa Deo non confusa' — this has a hymn cadence :

> Inter luctus cordis fluctus
> ludor, trudor horridos.
> Fera bella et duella
> Fluctus cient horridos
> Hinc rebelle me procella
> Abripit diluvium
> Monstra uana et profana
> agitant tripudium.

and is followed by a hymn of consolation in which Providentia and Justitia, together with Moses, David, Jonas, and angels comfort 'Gens Israel'.   The last act ends with a chorus divided among individual inhabitants of Bethulia and consisting of shouts of praise to Judith.   This is succeeded by the 'Epilogus', which (as in most of these dramas) emphasises the trumph and the moral in a stanza many times repeated : —

> Uicit Judith sonent plausus
> Superauit triumphauit, detruncauit
>   hostem strauit
> Dic triumphum laeta pubes
> ite noctes, ite nubes
>   dicite uictoriam.

A similar function of the Epilogue is evident in *Judith* (1650, Engelberger Klosterbibliothek) where a paean of praise is sung to Judith, in which angels, the leaders of the people and Joachim the High Priest take part, as do the Virgin and Christ in the following song.

---

1. Cp. the summaries of the arias sung by the Chorus in *Victrix fiducia Bethuliae* (Appendix A).

2. By the courtesy of the authorities at the Staatsbibliothek, München, I was able to examine this MS. and to use it for quotation.

Frequently the Epilogue consisted of a procession (sometimes immediately preceding the distribution of prizes) [1]. Sometimes the great performances were accompanied by festive processions through the streets, as in the 'Esther' drama played in Munich in 1577, when over 1700 persons took part in the procession [2]. Of a somewhat different kind is the Epilogue of *Tragoedia Mundi*, which succeeds a scene with allegorical figures : here an explanation and summary of the drama are given, apparently without musical aid, and more in the manner of the Protestant 'Schuldrama' :

> Holofernes ist spöttlich gstorben
> Judith hat den sig erworben
> Bethulia ist höchlich erfreut
> Jerusalem vergessen sleid
> Maria die nimbt Judith schwerdt
> Und gwint den sig und bherschet derd
> Religion nimbt oberhand
> den alten stand bhalt svatterland.

This is succeeded by a warning against the evils prophesied in the Old Testament and an exhortation to trust in the Blessed Virgin.

The chorus gradually lost in importance as time went on, and it was partially replaced by tourneys, dances, songs, or music alone [3]; while staging and decoration played an increasingly important part [4]. Parallel to the use of the chorus as a semi-alle-

---

1. v. *Juditha et Holofernes* (1654) : " Victoria & Triumphus Judithae transfertur in fortiorem hostium Debellatricam *Mariam*, quae cum in litterario quoque certamine palmam conferat, ideo triumphali ipsius Curru debita Victoribus praemia advehuntur.

Weil Juditha ein Vorbild unnd Abriss der unüberwindlichen glorwürdigsten Heldin und Jungkfrawen Mariae gewesen / also wird diser Bildnuss in einem Triumphwagen mit gebürender Ehr und Preyss herfür geführt / mit ihr als einem Sitz der Weissheit die Proemia, den Obsigern in den freyen Künsten ausszutheylen ".

2. v. B. Duhr S. J. *op. cit.* vol. I, p. 345.

3. v. N. Nessler : *Das Jesuitendrama in Tirol.* Ein Beitrag zur Geschichte des Schuldramas. LVI. Programm des K. K. Gymnasiums zu Brixen (1906), p. 35. This development is foreshadowed in the drama of *Judith* (1650, Engelberger Klosterbibliothek) where Acts III and IV close with a symphony (which in the former " precedit currum "). cp. also the use of the " Tanz " in *Judith* 1763 (Aachen) as a kind of symbolic dumb show to anticipate the action.

4. A description of a typical stage in the Academic College at Vienna is of interest in this connection : ' ...das Theatrum in seiner perspectiv, so schier grösser und länger alss das Auditorium selbst / und kann man die darin stehende scenas offterer alss 12 biss 13 mahl augenblicklich verendern... (v. Codex 8227 Wiener Hofbibliothek (Codex Testarello) pag. 739-829. quoted in J. Zeidler : *Die Schauspielthätigkeit der Schüler und Studenten Wiens.* 18. Programm des K. K. Staatsgymnasiums... in Oberhollabrun 1888, p. 39).

gorical figure in the Latin Jesuit dramas is the extensive use of omens and machinery. In the *Fiducia in Deum* of Avancinus this is particularly noticeable. In Act I (scene 4) the Assyrians, while cutting off the water supply from Bethulia, discover a tablet on which is engraven the story of Israel's deliverance out of Egypt (this device avoids Achior's long narrative of the Israelites) ; similarly in Act II (scene 6), when the citizens of Bethulia are gathering the rain water (which falls miraculously at the moment when Ozias returns a negative answer to the Assyrian challenge to surrender) they find an image of Moses ; and this is promptly acclaimed as a favourable omen. In the second scene of Act III tempests descend on those who counsel the surrender of the city, and Chermes, one of the Assyrian generals, is struck by lightning while blaspheming Jehovah. In the sixth scene of the same act a 'militia coelestis' disturbs the Assyrian camp ; and in Act IV angels appear to Judith to encourage her, and one of them throws an arrow with a message of hope into the beleaguered city. All this is merely extending into the action of the play what had already been implicit in many of the dramas. In the 'periocha' *Juditha et Holofernes* (1654) we find the following summary of Act II, scene 8, where Arrogantia and Fiducia argue : 'Der Hochmuth / weil er sich stoltz in die höhe erhebt / wirdt von Göttlicher Rach urblitzlich zu Boden geschlagen'. Similarly in *Victrix fiducia Bethuliae* (II. 4) Holofernes is warned in a dream of Sisera to beware of 'Betrug Weiblicher Nachstellung' ; and in Act III (scene 2) Bachus (*sic*) and Cupido triumph over him while he is asleep and 'machen dem Todt einen Zugang / ihme den Rest zugeben / wollen hierdurch andeuten / wie er durch eygne seine Laster seye umbkommen'. In the *Judith* of 1650 (Engelberger Klosterbibliothek) Judith holds converse with spirits (V. 2) including Sisera, Jael (who encourages her) and others. In all these and many other instances, the basic assumption is similar to that of Avancinus ; and although from a modern point of view such miraculous interventions are detrimental to dramatic characterisation, there is no doubt that in the 17th and 18th centuries they contributed to the popularity and success of the Judith plays.

It is evident that the Jesuits were practised playwrights ; they knew how to appeal to the taste of the audience in externals, and thus found ample opportunity for the fulfilment of their other aims. And another reason for the popularity of the Judith theme is indicated : it lent itself admirably to such staging, such musical and scenic effects, such an appeal to sympathy, reinforced by a religious doctrine excellently summarised in the chorus quoted above of 'Spes confisa Deo non confusa'.

Skilful technique is equally evident in the structure of many of the dramas. Here again there is a kind of pattern — that of the 'Jesuitenkomödie' in general. As may be seen from a consideration of the choruses, two separate actions can frequently be distinguished ; often one is biblical, the other mythological. Prologue and Epilogue demonstrate the connection between these two parallel actions. In the later dramas, the different Parts or Acts often contain an equal number of scenes [1] — gradually, from the comparative freedom of the earlier plays [2], there is a development to this rigid arrangement, which reappears as a characteristic both of opera and oratorio. Interludes, however, are often admitted ; sometimes they are included in the 'periocha' and their contents summarised. They seem either to have treated the subject in a comic way or to have been totally unconnected with it. It is noteworthy that throughout the Jesuit drama serious and comic scenes were intermingled in this manner. In the *Judith* of 1650, for example, a 'symphonia ludicra recitatio' occurs in the middle of a scene (IV. 2) ; in *Juditha et Holofernes* (1654) the following summary of a scene is given (III. 1) : 'Immitten als solche auffzuwarten abgerueffen / kombt ein vertrunckener Handwercksman seltsam auff die Binn / und in das spil'. Similarly in the fifth scene of Part III, an Assyrian officer finds the guard asleep 'den er mit Steckenklopffen endtlich auffgeweckt / und darauf Briglen lassen' ('ad fustuarium abstrahi jubet'). It is easy to recognise the Hans Wurst of the 'Volksschauspiel' who acts as messenger for Holofernes (v. infra p. 73).

While the Interlude proper was often unconnected with the subject, the 'scena muta' — another favourite device — was essentially linked with the action. It might be a pantomimic or symbolic scene, or it might represent a dream (as in *Victrix fiducia Bethuliae* II. 4). It is interesting to note that the Judith subject positively suggests a scena muta of the pantomimic kind, since the slaying of Holo-

---

1. e. g. *Judithae de Holoferne triumphus* (1720), where each of the three Parts contains 5 scenes and a final chorus.

2. e. g. *Juditha, et Holofernes* (1654) where the three Parts contain 6, 9, and 9 scenes respectively, and also *Victrix fiducia Bethuliae* where there are 7, 9 and 9.

fernes, if pourtrayed at all, must be of that nature. In the Luzern drama, *Tragoedia Mundi*, one of the few stage directions is as follows : 'sy nimbt ihn bi dem Kopf und schlag in 2 streich den Kopf ab' [1].

From a record of a Judith performance at Einsiedeln in 1676, it is evident that the whole drama was sometimes acted in dumb show [2] : 'Geschichte der Judith als scena muta. Am Rosenkranzsonntag bei der Prozession. Zuerst kniet die Heldin vor dem Zelt des Holofernes, der im prächtigen Zelte schlafend gesehen wurde. Zum Victoriagesang haut ihm Judith das Haupt ab und zeigt es dem Volke' [3]. The part was generally played by a boy, who recited a song of triumph as he cut off the head of Holofernes, the symbol of Evil [4].

The exposition in the Jesuit dramas on Judith is as a rule shorter than that of the other academic plays hitherto considered. In *Juditha et Holofernes* (1654) Judith appears in the sixth scene of the first Part ; the opening scenes are concerned with Holofernes and Achior, the cutting off of the water supply from Bethulia, the consequent revolt in the beleaguered city, and the decision of the elders

---

1. Cp. *Victrix fiducia Bethuliae* III. 3, where the action is similarly (or even more vividly) described.

2. v. Chronological Survey Nº 45.

3. v. P. G. Morel. in *Der Geschichtsfreund* vol. XVII, Einsiedeln, 1861, p. 103.

4. Ibid. (p. 91). The love of representing horrors is clearly shewn in these, as in most dumb shows. Soon the head of Holofernes was so contrived that blood ran from it. But the technical devices, it appears, were not always perfect ; the following incident is reported of the August performance of *Judith und Holofernes* at Einsiedeln in 1684 : ' " Als der Knabe dem schlafenden Holofernes den Schedel gescheitlet (weilen solches durch eine in Hals gesteckte Melunen zugericht ware), er die Melunen gar zu weit hinunter getrofen und deswegen der Hals einer ganzen Spanne lang worden: da benebens die Melunen gar weit vom Hals hinaus gesehen ; und vornemblich der noch übrige Theil mitsampt dem Kopf herfür gezogen, auf dem aufgerichteten Theatro oder Bühne herumgetrohlet, also dass ein Theil der Melunen auf der Bühne, der andere in dem Hals stecken gebliben, womit es mehr Lachens als Andachts gegeben ". Anlass zu diesem Spiele gaben wiederholte Siege der Christen über die Türken '. (P. G. Morel, *loc. cit.* pp.105-6.) P. G. Morel quotes from the Tagebuch of P. Joseph Dietrich, of Einsiedeln, in relating this incident. From the extracts from this diary published in *Mitteilungen des historischen Vereins des Kantons Schwyz* 22. Heft (Schwyz, 1911) it is evident that performances of biblical dramas or episodes were frequent, on the ' Rosenkranzsonntag ' especially, but also at other times (v. pp. 69, 71, 97, 99, 101, etc.). v. also W. Flemming : *Geschichte des Jesuitentheaters in den Landen deutscher Zunge*, Berlin, 1923. p. 172. for a discussion of ' künstliche Köpfe ' and of the head of Holofernes used in the drama of Avancinus.

to surrender if help does not come within five days.   Although only the scenario is preserved, it is evident from this summary that the exposition was concise and effective.   A slightly longer, but still concise exposition is to be found in the periocha of *Victrix fiducia Bethuliae* (1679).   Here Part I is taken up with Holofernes and Achior ; the reception of the latter's tale in the Assyrian camp, and the distress in Bethulia at his subsequent account of Holofernes are pourtrayed more in detail, and Part I ends with the mockery of the Assyrian soldiers when they have diverted the water supply from Bethulia.   This is a complete piece of exposition, expanding the title of Part I — 'Bethulia Pressa'.   Judith appears in the first scene of Part II ; she reproaches the Elders for lack of faith and gives them confidence — an appropriate opening to the second Part, which is entitled 'Bethulia Erecta'.   Even less exposition is to be found in the drama *Judithae de Holoferne triumphus* (1720). Part I (Bethulia Pressa) consists of five scenes, shewing Holofernes in his camp, 'victoriis tumidus', awaiting the surrender of Bethulia, the refusal of the city to comply with his demands, the tale of Achior and his banishment, and finally his entry into Bethulia as a captive. In the opening scene of Part II (Bethulia Relevata) Judith is seen descending from Bethulia into the camp of Holofernes, and conversing with Abra on her plans.   This is an instance of dramatic concentration remarkable among the Judith plays of this type and period ; Judith's part in the deliberations in Bethulia is omitted but is indicated by her conversation with her maid ;   while the general situation in Bethulia is indirectly pourtrayed in the dialogue between Holofernes and his generals (Part II scene 3) immediately before Judith's arrival at the camp ('Bethulia fontes perdidit et sicco obstinat...').   Each Part in this drama consists of five scenes ; Part II gives the development of the situation up to Holofernes' permission to Judith to pray outside the camp, and her prayer to God for strength ; Part III shews the summons to the banquet itself, the beheading of Holofernes and Judith's prayer, her exit from the camp and return to Bethulia, the fear and lamentations of the Assyrians on discovering the death of Holofernes, the flight of the enemy and the victorious rejoicings of the Hebrews.

In view of the similarity of structure between this play and the scenarios of other Jesuit dramas on Judith, it is reasonable to suppose that the execution may also have been similar.   It is of interest therefore to consider the drama of 1720 in some detail from a technical point of view. The author has great feeling for a dramatic situation ; this is particularly noticeable in Part II, scene 3, where Judith's arrival at the camp is exactly timed to allay Holofernes' growing impatience at the absence of any word from Bethulia, and where her flattery of him corresponds to the demonstration of his accessibility to flattery in his previous conversation with his generals. The short, divided dialogues throughout are doubtless evidence of a pedagogic intention (to give as many pupils as possible parts to speak seems to have been a primary aim of the Jesuit dramatists) ; but they also contribute very much to the dramatic effect of the play. The fifth scene of Part II, where Judith, having obtained permission of egress from the camp, goes out to pray, and the scene of the banquet in Part III, both afford examples of lively dramatic dialogue. The scenes in Part III (3 and 4) which shew the crisis of the action, are both effectively conceived. While Holofernes, intoxicated and helpless, is lying in his tent, and Judith is revolving in her mind the deed that she must do, soldiers sing a cheerful chorus in praise of wine and war :

> Sunt martis gaudia, magnanimorum jubila.
> Sunt mentis jubila martis solatia.
> Sunt mentis jubila martis solatia.
>   solatia et gaudia.
> Sunt mentis jubila la la la la etc.

> Abite tristia curarum ite nubila
> Jam Bacchus arida foecundat pectora
> Sunt vina mellea cordis solatia
>   tripudia, diludia
> et mentis ludicra cra cra cra cra etc.

Judith prays for strength, and when she emerges from the tent she gives the head of Holofernes to the trembling Abra. After reassuring the latter, she leaves the camp, replying to the challenge of the sentries (a dramatic moment) 'amicam cernis'. The next scene shews her return to Bethulia, and the fear of the Assyrians, who try to wake Holofernes, (invoking Aurora and Phoebus meanwhile). The discovery of his fate is received with lamentations ; here indeed we find an effective scene in almost every version of the story, for the language of the Book of Judith is itself dramatic : 'Holofernes iacet in terra et caput eius non est in illo'. The distribution of the cries, however, and the sudden dramatic moment when a soldier shouts 'Mulier !' are worth noting in this play, for they shew considerable technical mastery.

Much is made throughout of the big scenes — those of Holofernes and his generals, Judith and Holofernes at the banquet (where the feasting and revelry are pourtrayed with a delight almost equal to that of the old heroic poems) and Judith with the people of Bethulia, when they sing praises to her. But there is also a striking use of dialogue : the Assyrian soldiers and the Bethulian citizens play a great part in the Achior scenes, and it is the Assyrian chiefs who create the greatest impression of Judith's charm in the scene following her appearance. Apart from these scenes and the choruses, the main movement of the play is in the dialogue between Achior and Holofernes, and in the trial of wits between Judith and Holofernes. As a whole the drama is well constructed and concise, and though a late example, it shews the Jesuit drama at its best [1].

The Jesuit drama catered essentially for a large number of actors, of whom a few (the more gifted pupils) should have important rôles. Here again the subject of Judith shews itself suitable. The

---

[1]. Interesting evidence for the technical skill of the Jesuit dramatists is to be gathered from a copy of Sixt Birck's *Judith. Drama Comico-tragicum* (Coloniae, 1544) in the Staatsbibliothek, München. The copy evidently belonged to the Jesuit College in Munich, for ' Collegij Societatis Jesu Monachij ' is inserted in script below the title; In the same hand are the marginal corrections, excisions, and stage directions throughout. Some phrases are obviously altered for doctrinal purposes (e. g. ' simplex fides ' (I. 1) to ' cum firma spe ', and ' Lex atque scripta prophetarum funditus ' (I. 1) to ' Moris boni, pietas, obedientia, castitas, Et id genus reliquae virtutis funditus ', ' Sacerdos ' to ' Pontifex ' (I. 3), ' poenitentia vera ' (I. 5) to 'poenitentia aspera ', ' Nam maxime his placatur ipse victimis Nec gratius sacrum (si psalmis credimus Davidicis) quam vitae poenitentia ' (II. 4) to ' Nam maxime his placatur ipse victimis Si corporis non desit cas[ti]gatio '. Similarly, ' Nam gratitudo plus valet Apud Deum rebus secundis, quam pium Supplexque votum, cum premit necessitas ' (V. 11) is cut altogether). But there are also numerous excisions which indicate the practised actor-manager, cutting the over-lengthy speeches of Sixt Birck's drama. In I. 5, where Joachim in a long speech combining exposition with exhortation urges the Bethulians to fortitude, 79 lines are marked as if to be cut ; in II. 3, where Achior narrates the history of the Jews, 62 lines are similarly marked ; in III. 5, (the consultation of the Senate) 204 lines, some from each speech, are marked ; in II. 6, 30 lines, and in the following scene 22 lines ; in III. 11, 29 lines, in IV. 1, 66 lines, in IV. 2, 36 lines and in IV. 6, 26 lines (a repetition by Judith of Achior's previous narrative) are marked—apart from other minor omissions throughout. Stage directions — almost entirely lacking in the Latin drama of Sixt Birck (v. supra p. 46)—are also added in the margin, notably in the scene where Judith is summoned to the banquet and in V. 5 (' suspenditur caput '). The dramatis personae are altered, by omissions, additions, and substitutions. In particular, Hebrew and Assyrian characters are substituted for characters with classical names.

The copy is thus of considerable interest, shewing, as it appears to do, the ingenuity of the Jesuit dramatist in the adaptation of a Protestant play to his purpose.

number of Assyrians and Bethulians could be multiplied at will ; the senators of Bethulia, and the generals of Holofernes, could be made into smaller or bigger parts as circumstances suggested ; while the main rôles — Judith, Holofernes, Achior, Abra, Ozias and Joachim — gave scope for practice in acting, rhetoric and elocution. The periochae always contain at the end the names of the actors opposite the list of dramatis personae ; in one (*Juditha et Holofernes*, 1654) the names of 81 actors appear in the Syllabus Actorum ; in another (*Victrix fiducia Bethuliae*) 113 actors, together with 14 Personae musicae (allegorical characters), appear. In the MSS. or printed copies of dramas, the number of actors is not specified, apart from the principal characters, but it is evident from the text of *Tragoedia Mundi* (1647) and of *Judith* (1650, Engelberg) that it must have been large. The actors were usually the scholars of the 'Syntax', 'Humanist', and 'Rhetoric' classes ; sometimes there were others from the lower classes [1].

It is clear that from a formal point of view, the Jesuit dramas on the subject of Judith mark an advance on those previously considered. The important question remains : how far is any difference to be found in the conception of character and in the presentation of the story ? With one exception (*Judithae de Holoferne triumphus*, 1720) it may be said that the differences in characterisation are slight ; they do nevertheless convey an impression of greater skill and more alert dramatic sense. In its main outlines the narrative is of course identical in all the dramas of this period, since they follow closely the Apocryphal account. But some differences of emphasis on various traits of character are to be found. Judith herself is always firm of purpose, but in one drama (*Juditha et Holofernes* 1654, I. 6) she is strengthened by the examples of 'Heylige Vorfahrer' when sad at the lack of faith in Bethulia, while in others (*Tragoedia Mundi* 1647, II. 2, and *Judith* 1650, Engelberg, II. 6) she is represented as unwavering in her faith from the beginning and needing no such encouragement. In *Tragoedia Mundi*, however, she expresses a consciousness of her own unworthiness for so great a task :

> Ich ein sündhaffte Dienerin
> Vor minem got und Heren
> Zu gering und schlecht ich bin,
> In würdig zu verehren'   (II, 2).

---

1. e-g. Chronological Survey N° 56.

At the same time she is sufficiently resolute and self-contained not to communicate anything of her plan to the priests, beyond the fact that she is determined to go out to the Assyrian camp.

Stress is frequently laid upon her beauty and virtue, and upon her widowhood (the last point is emphasised in the Apocryphal version and is of interest in view of Hebbel's discussion of this motive, v. infra p. 97). In *Juditha et Holofernes* (1654, 'Summarischer Inhalt') she is thus described : '... wirdt Edle / Reiche / an Tugend und Leibsgestalt über alle fürtreffliche Fraw / Judith genannt / so ihres Alters bey 30 Jahren / keusch unnd heilig im Wittibstandt lebte / von Gott angetriben / für ihren Glauben und liebes Vatterlandt zustreitten.... [1]' This summary of her character is matched in the *Judith* of 1650 (Engelberg) by the opening scene of Act I, in which allegorical figures (Castitas, Timor Dei etc.) stress Judith's piety against the arguments of other figures (Opulentia, Voluptas etc.). In *Judithae de Holoferne triumphus* (1720), however, there is notable advance in characterisation. All direct summary of Judith's character is omitted, even in Praeludium and Chorus ; her first appearance is unheralded, and she is seen in action, descending with Abra to the Assyrian camp. From her conversation it is plain that she is following the divine command : 'diriget gressum Deus'. In compensation for such dramatic concentration, this play expands, more than others, the adroitness of Judith's treatment not only of Holofernes, but of his soldiers, and of all with whom she has dealings. 'Nullus insidiis locus', she says to the Assyrian sentries :

' Amica gerimus corda, qua pacem petant '.

One of her audience counters this immediately :

' Suspecta res est : foeminae nulla est fides ' ;

and a lively discussion of some length follows, during which Judith persuades them of her innocence.

'Quid una tantis foemina illudet viris ?', she asks, with instinctive appreciation of their appetite for flattery ; the distrustful sentry, it is true, answers :

' Saepe una magnis foemina illusit viris '

---

[1]. A similar description is in the Argumentum of *Victrix fiducia Bethuliae* (1679) (v. Appendix A.).

and 'laus fraus muliebra sunto' ; but Judith convinces the majority, and so is led to Holofernes, where she has on the whole an easier task. For there is in this play a distinct attempt to represent the character of Holofernes on its most vulnerable side. He is shewn, in the first scene, to be more than usually accessible to flattery. The dramatist describes him as 'Victoriis tumidus' in the stage direction ; but not content with this, he devotes some time to shewing the effect on Holofernes of the adulation of his generals :

> ' mihi vestra proceres vota et affectus placent ;
> placet meorum pompa regalis ducum... '   (I, I)

Moreover, he is correspondingly impatient of obstacles ; and at the end of the first scene, effectively placed as final contrast to the general atmosphere of flattery, the one obstacle to his complete triumph is recounted :

> ' Bethulia portas claudit, et menʒəm obstinat '.

On the arrival of the message from Bethulia with its refusal to surrender, he mocks at Israel and Israel's God, and a dramatic outburst against the audacity of the Bethulians greets Achior's attempt to turn his purpose. The next picture of Holofernes is at the moment of Judith's arrival (II. 3). He is all impatience, and in the conversation of the generals the parlous state of Bethulia is indicated. So he receives her graciously, and she, on her side, knows how to flatter him. He responds to her every lure ; she finds grace in his eyes, and he accedes to all her requests.

There is here a definite attempt to motivise the action of Holofernes in yielding to Judith with such careless ease, and although the Chorus and Israel's Genius emphasise the orthodox explanation of the judgment of God, one cannot but feel that the author also wished to shew that judgment fulfilled through character. Slight as is the attempt, it strikes a note more akin to modern feeling than anything in the characterisation of Holofernes in other Jesuit dramas. In these, he is drawn as an arrogant tyrant, quick to anger against Achior and full of cruel designs against Bethulia. But it is not altogether easy to reconcile this figure, the Holofernes of the opening scenes, with the victim of Judith's first approach — though it is easy later to account for his fall through the influence of wine and passion. Most of the dramatists did not concern themselves with this difficulty ; the divine aid granted to Judith on behalf of Bethulia explained it all [1]. Here, in the 1720 *Judith*, an explanation is at least indicated, and there is some warrant for regarding this attempt as a link between the mediaeval and the modern conception of the tale.

All the dramas inspired by didactic aims (however much concealed these aims may be by technical skill and dramatic interest) agree in their treatment of Judith's victory as an entirely satisfactory issue. No sympathy for Holofernes is visible in any one of them. The most that can be done for him is to ignore him at the end, and to concentrate on the joyful victory of Bethulia and the oppressed ; the moment that comment is made on his fate, it is necessarily of an adverse character. Such, for example, is the symbolic scene in *Juditha et Holofernes* (1654) : 'Diuina Nemesis & Fiducia fustis poenis impios Holofernis manes deuouent' (III.8). In this respect the dramatic versions, until the 19th century, shew the same attitude as the Old English heroic poem, where the soul of Holofernes is consigned to 'þām heolstran hām hyhtwynna lēas'. But whereas Judith, in the older versions, accepts as her right the spoils and plunder offered to her as trophies from the Assyrian camp, and dedicates them, as in the biblical version, to the Lord, a more ascetic trait occasionally appears in the Jesuit dramas. In *Victrix fiducia Bethuliae* she refuses the 'ansehlichen Raub' which is offered her (III. 9). In other plays, the incident was used symbolically, as in *Judith* (1650, Engelberg), where the Assyrian spoils are handed to Judith as the prizes are distributed to the scholars. In others again, the question is evaded by omission of the external signs of victory, which are neglected in the songs of praise and thanksgiving. The old heroic delight in them has yielded to the ascetic idea of incongruity between spiritual aid and material gain.

The minor characters in the tale are for the most part still lifeless. There is little variation in the part played by Achior, save perhaps in the length of his speeches. He invariably incurs the anger of Holofernes by his long account of Jewish history, is exiled, bound to a tree (this effective stage detail survives in every version) [2], is

1. In one play, even the warning dreams of his ' Götzenpriester' are made unavailing by the grace of God (*Victrix fiducia Bethuliae* II. 4 and II. 8). Apart from the drama of 1720, one of the best versions of Holofernes' fall is in the outline of the action in the periocha of *Judith* (1763, Aachen) II. 6 & 7. v. Appendix B.

2. In the English version of the apocryphal book he is bound and ' cast down at the foot of the hill' (VI. 13.) but in the Vulgate the verse runs : Illi autem, divertentes

found by the Bethulians and taken before the Elders. In some of the plays, his conversion to the Jewish faith is shewn, in accordance with the apocryphal version, after the victory of the Bethulians (as in *Victrix fiducia Bethuliae* III, 8., where the juxtaposition, in the same scene, of Achior's conversion and the mockery hurled by the Bethulian youths at the head of Holofernes is taken over from the Apocrypha and is characteristic of the Old Testament conception). Occasionally, as in *Judith* (1650, Engelberg) Achior plays an individual part in the rejoicings which greet Judith's victory [1]; but in other dramas (as in *Judithae de Holoferne Triumphus*) the figure, after providing an important part of the exposition in Act I, is allowed to drop out of the action imperceptibly.

The only other minor characters worthy of remark are Abra and Vagao [2]. Abra is, as a rule, a silent and unimportant figure, present only for stage purposes (to receive the head of Holofernes and to accompany Judith on her expedition) and as a foil to Judith's courage. Occasionally however she is accounted worthy of description; Judith's 'O fida serva' in the Engelberg drama of 1650 (III, 4,) shews appreciation of her distinctive quality. [In this play indeed her rôle is more definite than usual, both in the preparations (III. 2) and at the crisis, where her hesitation throws up Judith's fears, which are dispelled by a vision of Jael (V. 2)].

In *Tragoedia Mundi* her freedom is proclaimed with Judith's to the army at the end of the Judith action (II. 8) — an unusual recognition of her services [3].

Vagao is even more shadowy in the majority of the dramas. But he too is sometimes more individual and dramatic — as indeed he is in the original apocryphal tale — in the scene where he discovers

---

a latere montis ligaverunt Achior ad arborem manibus et pedibus ; et sic vinctum restibus dimiserunt eum, et reversi sunt ad dominum suum.

1. T. B. Aldrich, in search of dramatic motives to enrich the action, expands this trait in Achior and shews him in love with Judith. v. infra p. 115. A hint for this might be found in the Book of Judith XIV. 7-8, although no suggestion but that of admiration and reverence is made there.

2. Vagao is the form of the Vulgate, Bagoas that of the Lutheran translation of the Bible (as of the English A. V.). The forms Pagoa (Hans Sachs) and Bagos (Opitz) are of course variants of the second form. The name appears as Vagao in the Jesuit dramas.

3. Cp. also M. Böhme's *Tragicomœdia*, where Judith sets Abra free (v, 4), and the appropriate moral is pointed in the Epilogue :

     Lehrt das man geb dem Gesindel Lohn /
     Wenns uns hat lieb und trew gethon.

Holofernes lying dead. His speech of lamentation in the *Judith* of 1650 (Engelberg) is effective (V. 5.) [1] ; but in other dramas this, the sole dramatic part of Vagao's rôle, is assigned to several Assyrian soldiers (e. g. *Judithae de Holoferne Triumphus* III. 4).

The Jesuit dramas tend in general to distribute what action there is, apart from the main characters, among representatives of a crowd — e. g. the officers of Holofernes (*Tragoedia Mundi* I. 3, II, 7., *Judith* (1650) I. 3, 4, and 5, II, 3, IV, 2., *Judithae de Holoferne Triumphus* I. 1, II. 3, III. 2, etc.), the Assyrian soldiers (*Judithae de Holoferne Triumphus* II. 2, III. 1 — where the cook enumerates with relish the dishes and wines for the banquet — III.5, *Juditha et Holofernes* (1654) II. 3, III. 3, etc.), the Bethulian citizens (*Judith* (1650) I. 6, II. 2, V. 3-4, *Victrix fiducia Bethuliae* I. 4, I.6, II. 7, III. 5, etc.). Sometimes a representative minor figure appears, as the Wachtmeister in *Victrix fiducia Bethuliae* (III. 4), the disillusioned 'Spectator 3' of *Judithae de Holoferne Triumphus* (II.2), or the Cook and Hofmeister of Holofernes' camp (*Tragoedia Mundi* II. 8, *Judithae de Holoferne Triumphus* III. 1). This characteristic was no doubt partly due to a desire to distribute the minor rôles as evenly as possible, and to create the impression of lively dialogue and crowd scenes ; it is further evidence of the technical adroitness of the Jesuit dramatists.

The plays of the Jesuits exercised, as is now recognised, a great influence on popular drama, or the 'Volksschauspiel'. Performances for the benefit of the populace were of course common long before the development of scholastic plays ; the very origins of mediaeval drama must be sought in popular representations of the Christian mysteries. But on the decay of the Passion Plays in South Germany and Austria (after the great Bozen Play of 1514), other biblical subjects were substituted ; tales of Old Testament heroes, the lives of Saints and Martyrs, and finally historical events, became the common themes of the 'Volksschauspiel', and it is in these especially that the influence of the 'Jesuitenkomödie' may be traced [2]. Among the subjects of representation in the valleys of Tirol the theme of Judith seems to have enjoyed some favour. A performance is recorded at Vomperfeld in the 16th century, and 200 years later

1. Cp. also the outline of this scene in *Victrix fiducia Bethuliae* (III. 7) (Appendix A).

2. v. A. Sikora ; *Zur Geschichte der Volksschauspiele in Tirol* (Separatabdruck aus dem Archiv für Theatergeschichte vol. II. pp. 1-55) pp. 9 and 13.

(1770) another at Afing in the valley of the Sarn [1]. Similarly, in 1604, a performance of *Judith* is recorded at Freiburg i / Breisgau ; and there is no doubt that the 'shows' and plays represented on festival days in the processions were in the nature of 'Volksschauspiele' [2]. Reference has already been made to the pantomimic representations of Judith's victory over Holofernes which were organised and carried out by the Rosenkranzbrüderschaft during these processions. They are essentially akin to the 'Volksschauspiel', and even shew an exploitation of the popular love of horrors in the interests of religious propaganda. The popular plays expanded the melodramatic element in the story, and used more extensively the devices, already noted in the Jesuit plays, of Interlude, comic dialogue, and spectacular scene.

All these are to be found in a late specimen of popular play, published by A. Schlossar in *Deutsche Volksschauspiele* In Steiermark gesammelt [3]. The play is printed from a MS. in Graz, and a reference to Maria Theresia in the concluding lines points to the years 1760-1770 as its probable date. The most interesting feature of this popular version is the introduction of Hans Wurst as the messenger. Scenes of communication (between Nabucodonosor and Holofernes, Holofernes and Bethulia, Holofernes and Judith etc.) are therefore multiplied. The old disregard for change of scene is entirely gone ; in its place appears the stage direction 'Verwandlung', or even more frequently that for the use of the drop-curtain ('Zwischenvorhang'). The stock-in-trade of Hans Wurst, as usual, consists in the use of dialect, puns, and garbled forms of names and words. Achior is referred to as 'Herr Aichhorn', Holofernes as 'Herr Oxferna' ; the scene in which the death of Holofernes is discovered has become pure farce : 'Der Herr Oxferna liegt drin, er hat kein Haupt, kein Kopf und kein Schädel, dös hat g'wiss than die Sakraments hebräische Gredl' (sc. 27). Liberty is of course allowed to Hans Wurst to speak more than is set down for him. The stage direction in scene 10 is as follows : 'Achior wird an einen Baum gebunden. Hier kann eine Vorstellung mit Singen gemacht werden. Es kann auch der Hans Wurst mit Achior eine Rede führen' ; and in the banquet scene (sc. 22) even more explicitly : 'Sie trinken Gesundheit, es wird auch Musik gemacht. Es kann auch, so man will, der Hans

---

1. v. Chronological Survey Nos. 19 and 70.
2. v. Chronological Survey Nos. 45, 48, 53, 55.
3. vol. II, pp. 1-38. v. Chronological Survey, No. 68.

Wurst Spässe machen' (so the printed edition: the MS., according to a note, has 'das Seinige thun'). Apart from the dialect of the comic scenes, and from the passages in which the language is directly biblical, the style is inflated and full of circumlocution, in the favourite manner of the 'Haupt=und Staatsaktion'. Nabuco- donosor — the most imperious tyrant who ever appeared on a fairy-tale stage — issues commands to his generals in the opening scene, and they are received with general agreement : 'Dero Befehl, Ihro königliche Majestät, seien wir alle bereitet, genauesten Vollzug zu leisten'. Holofernes, receiving Judith with great favour, makes her long and complimentary speeches, in which he praises her 'angenehmen Wort' and 'schöne Zierlichkeiten', that cause his heart to be flooded with passion. ('O unerträgliche Liebe !', he says in an aside : 'Mein Herz brennt in vollem Feuer' sc. 20.), They indulge in reciprocal politenesses in the banquet scene, Holofernes saying 'Keineswegs gebeten, sondern nur befohlen !', which is countered by Judith with: 'dahero nur befohlen, was beliebt, und nicht gebeten'. (sc. 22).

The construction of the play is neater and more effective than its language would suggest. The first five scenes shew the tyrant Nabucodonosor challenging the surrounding countries, and the con- sequent orders to Holofernes to burn and ravage without mercy. Scenes 6 to 9 shew alternately (by means of the drop curtain) the fear of Holofernes in Bethulia, his ruthless refusal of mercy to the messenger from the city, and the measures taken to garrison the town, mountains and frontier. (The influence of 17th and 18th century warfare on the drama is plain). Scenes 9 to 11 are devoted to Achior. One slight detail may be noted as an addition : Achior is referred to by Samuel as the man ' der vor etlichen Jahren bei uns gewohnt hat ' (sc. 10). Scene 12 is very brief, and shews Holofernes sending Felix to cut off water from Bethulia ; the drop curtain is again used, and scenes 13 and 14 pourtray the distress in Bethulia and the revolt of the citizens, ending in the decision to surrender in five days. In the 15th scene Judith enters ; this and the three following scenes shew her reproaching the Elders (in lengthy speeches), praying for strength, preparing for her attempt, and arriving at the camp of Holofernes. In her prayer she reveals her plan—no doubt a concession to popular feeling, which might otherwise be bewildered or offended by her actions. (Em- phasis is laid in the stage directions on the beauty of her apparel, and she is addressed on her exit as ' wertheste Frau Judith '). The 19th scene shews Holofernes in his tent, impatient at the absence of news from the Israelites, and thus well prepared for Judith's entry, which follows in the next scene.   She is introduced by Hans Wurst (formerly the messenger from Jerusalem, who has entered the service of Holofernes) and Holofernes at once receives her graciously and falls hopelessly in love with her.   In the following scene Judith rejoices at the impression she has made, but cautions Abra to be wary.   She is then summoned by Hans Wurst to the banquet, and the drop curtain rises and shews her arrival at the table.   She eats and drinks of her own provisions, but easily induces Holofernes to excess.   In scene 23 there is a change of setting ; the bed of Holofernes projects on to the stage so that he can be half seen by the audience.   Judith and Abra together emerge from the back of the stage, and in an explicit address Judith satisfies the morals of the audience : ' Gott sei abermal Dank, ich habe den vollgezechten Hauptmann Holofernes zur Ruhestatt begleitet, und Gott hat es gegeben, sobald er sich in das Bett niedergelegt, ist er augenblicklich entschlafen, damit ich, o Gott, deine Magd an der Ehre nicht beleidigt werde '.   This emphatic assertion is character-istic of the Volksschauspiel, which shares with the fairy tale its regard for technical morality.   Judith then prays for fortitude, and the stage direction indicates the 'scena muta ' : ' Es wird eine Vorstellung gemacht, als schlüge die Judith mit dem Schwert dem Holofernes im Bett das Haupt ab '.   A kind of chorale accompanies the pantomime, until Judith appears from behind the partition with the blood-stained head, and gives thanks to God.   Scenes 24 to 26 shew the rejoicings in the beleaguered city, and the part taken in them by Achior ; in the next scene Hans Wurst tries to waken Holofernes, but finds him dead ; the Assyrians flee, after a mimic battle with three adversaries on each side, and in the final scene praise and thanksgiving rise from Bethulia in a prayer with a contem-porary application :

> ' Weiter, o Gott, wir auch bitten than,
> Für unsre Landesmutter fein,
> Wann sie die Feind ' thun greifen an
> Thu unser Helfer sein.
> Wir kommen auch zu beten :
> O thu uns all' erretten,
> Damit dein Nam auf dieser Erd
> Allzeit geheiligt werd. '

Here all the elements of the Jesuit drama are to be found, together with the topical application of the older Reformers, and the specifically popular addition of the figure of Hans Wurst in comic scenes. The play is of great value as evidence for the influence of Jesuit scholastic drama (in subject and in treatment) on the drama of the people. It is of interest also as shewing how those features which were associated with the ' Haupt=und Staatsaktionen ' of the early 18th century in reality survived in popular drama, and notably in the treatment of a biblical subject originally popularised by the influence of religious and scholastic plays.

A cursory glance at this specimen of popular drama would suffice to establish its relation to the Puppet Play and its two descendants— the marionette theatre and the Punch and Judy show. It is not surprising therefore to find a record of ' Judith und Holofernes ' as a favourite subject of the puppet theatre in Hamburg in 1785 [1]. Nor was the subject neglected in England ; *Judith and Holofernes* appears to have been frequently given at Bartholomew's Fair in the 17th and 18th centuries [2]. In 1732 we find the *Siege of Bethulia* played as a favourite show on Lee and Harper's stage at the Fair, and engravings were made of the characteristic scene shewing Judith brandishing a sword and displaying the head of Holofernes [3]. That comic scenes formed an integral part of these shows is evident from the letter-press accompanying such engravings : ' The Droll of the *Siege of Bethulia*, containing the Ancient History of Judith and Holofernes, with the Comical Humours of Rustego and his Man Terrible ' [4]. The Punch and Judy shows must be lineally descended from such plays.

It has been already noted that the religious drama in Germany, under the influence of the Jesuits, developed in the direction of musical and decorative representations of biblical themes. The ' Ludi Caesarei ' performed before the court (especially in Vienna, Prague,

---

1. H. M. Schletterer : *Das deutsche Singspiel*. Augsburg, 1863, p. 229.

2. Locke writes in 1664 (of a Christmas scene in the church at Cleves) : ' Had they but given them motion it had been a perfect Puppet Play... for they were of the same size and make that our English puppets are ; and, I am confident, these shepherds and this Joseph are kin to that Judith and Holophernes which I had seen at Bartholomew Fair '. v. *Memoirs of Bartholomew Fair*, by H. Morley. London, 1859, p. 242. Pepys also saw a *Holofernes*, (v. Chronological Survey Nos. 61, and 42).

3. v. Chronological Survey No. 61.

4. v. *Memoirs of Bartholomew's Fair* loc. cit.

Graz, and Innsbruck) were particularly rich in scenic decoration and musical adornment, and appear to form a link between the later Jesuit drama and the Italian opera which in Southern Germany was its most formidable rival [1]. For meanwhile a parallel development of the courtly drama into a highly decorated ' dramma per musica ' was taking place in Italy; and from the early 17th century onwards, some of the taste for light musical ornament, gallant love-making and mythological subjects, penetrated into Germany. Singing ballet, ' Schäferspiel ' and other experiments were all combined in the opera or ' Singspiel '; and in 1627 Opitz's translation of Rinuccini's *Dafne* marked the beginning of the operatic era in Germany. So great was the influence of Italy, however, that by the early 18th century Italian Grand Opera had almost entirely supplanted the native ' Singspiel ' [2]. Only in Hamburg was the attempt made to continue the latter. Musical plays on biblical subjects were produced there, and an endeavour at compromise

---

1. v. J. Zeidler : *Studien und Beiträge zur Geschichte der Jesuitenkomödie und des Klosterdramas*, ed. cit. pp. 26-27.

' Sing = Comödien ' or dramatic oratorios appear in the course of the 17th century and precede the regular opera; while the introduction of women to play female rôles seems also to have led in the direction of opera, as may be gathered from the following extract from *Historia Collegii S. J. Oenipontani*. Ex libris originalibus manuscriptis... fideliter excerpta a. 1813. p. 39 (z. J. 1704. d. 1ten May). (MS. Bibliothek Museum Ferdinandeum Innsbruck Nr. 596) : ' cavendum est, ne deinceps foeminae producantur in theatrum, quod hic iam *tertio* factum, ipsis secularibus admirantibus rem alioquin ab uso nostro abhorrentem, praesertim vero non permittendum, ut id genus themata diligantur et more italico pertractentur intermixtis amoribus profanis fientque nostra dramata ad instar Italicorum, quas Operas vocant, ut parum ab ils differant nostra, nisi quod latino sermone haec constent ; de reliquo contexantur perinde, ut illa involutionibus amatoriis erroribusque e [iusdem] m[ateriae] fuit haec Aglae et nuper Margarita de Cortona atque ante biennium alia similis, commendatae quidem a spectatoribus tum materiae nobis hactenus non usitatae, tum artis scenicae seculari stylo aptatae. Sed praestat non recedero a gravitate in scenis nostris hactenus commendata et secularibus concedere, ut laudem ferant, quam decet nos declinare ac spernere... (quoted by Professor K. Lechner *op. cit.* pp. 88-9). The connection between scholastic drama and opera is made clear in the *Theatrophania* of Christophorus Rauch (1682) and the *Dramatologia* of Pastor Elmenhorst (1688). [v. Emil Riedel : *Schuldrama und Theater* in *Aus Hamburgs Vergangenheit*. herausgeg. K. Koppmann. Hamburg u. Leipzig 1885. p. 185.]

2. This influence seems to have extended even to oratorio. The *Giuditta* oratorio of Al. Scarlatti was performed (with Italian and German text in 4⁰) in Vienna in 1695 ; that of C. Ag. Badia in 1710, and that of Gius. Porsile in 1723. Metastasio's *Betulia Liberata* was performed in 1733 and in 1740. The oratorios on *Giuditta* of Giov. Freschi and A. Draghi were also performed (but the scores have no dates attached). v. A. v. Weilen : *Zur Wiener Theatergeschichte* (Schriften des österreichischen Vereins für Bibliothekswesen) Wien, 1901, pp. 50, 73, 87, 103, 111, & 117.

between the two different styles was made ; but in 1730 (after a period of success lasting from about 1696 to 1718) the Hamburg Opera house had to close down.

The *Judith* of Martin Opitz in 1635 thus belongs to the first stage in the development of German opera. It is called a ' biblical drama ', but it shews the characteristic features of an operatic text. The use of choruses in lyric measures, already noted in the scholastic dramas of the 16th century, is carried much further ; the chorus of the captive kings, of the watch and the soldiers, of the Hebrews, and of the Hebrew maidens, obviously fulfil the function of arias, following on the dialogue which is often in the nature of recitative. The allusions to Venus, Mars, and Bacchus made by the soldiers of Holofernes (the expression of Opitz's passion for classical learning) confirm the impression that the opera preserves some traits of the scholastic drama :

> ' Wie blicken doch aus ihrer Lufft herfür
> Der Mars und Venus Stern !
> Die Judith gleicht der Venus selbst an Zier
> Und Mars ist Holofern '.　　　　　　　(ii, 4).

More significant still is the fact that the action (which plunges in medias res, on the third day after Judith's arrival at the Assyrian camp) opens with a love-plaint of Holofernes, lamenting his passion for Judith in the conventional accents of Romance lovers :

> ' Aber, ach ! ich kan ja siegen :
> Doch, was hilft es, dass die Hand
> Zähmet so viel Leut ' und Land,
> Und das Hertze muss erliegen,
> Muss sich lassen jetzt bekriegen,
> Nicht durch strenge Schlacht und Streit,
> Sondern schöne Freundlichkeit,
> Kein starckes Heer hat mich
> 　　　Gejaget je zurücke,
> 　　　Jetzt zitter' ich
> Für einem leichten Augenblicke.
> Es muste mein Gebot so mancher König spüren,
> Jetzt aber kan ich selbst mich nicht regieren.
> . . . .
> ...O ja sie ists allein ! diss Reden, dieses Lachen,
> Der Augen Unstern ists, der mein Gesicht entzückt,
> Das Haar, das mein Gemüth, und allen Muth bestrickt,
> Der Mund, der meinen Mund kein gantzes Wort läst machen. '
> 　　　　　　　　　　　　　　　　　(i, 1).

If Holofernes is an operatic hero, consumed by passion and brought low by guile, Judith is no less an operatic heroine. Her address to the sun in the second scene of Act I at once creates the impression of a prima donna :

> ' Sonne, Zier der Erde,
> Die du zur Nachtruh schreitest,
> Und die müden Pferde
> In die See zum Trincken reitest ;
> Zürne nicht, dass du mich siehst
> In des rauen Volckes Händen,
> Das ein Feind des Höchsten ist... '

It is parallelled by Holofernes' address to the moon in the first scene of Act II, which shews him still more decisively as the love-lorn hero :

> ' O Judith, wann ich dich zu schauen nicht vermag,
> Ist ohne Monden Nacht, und ohne Sonne Tag ! '

The presentation of Judith's character is of necessity cursory, but Opitz is not altogether sympathetic to his heroine. Indeed, his whole conception of the two principal characters is alien from the spirit of the Germanic poems and dramas hitherto considered. The courtly love-making and gallantry shew an incursion of Romance ideals ; and it is not surprising to learn from Opitz's Preface that he adapted the play from an Italian source [1].

There are only three acts—a feature which may be traced to the operatic tradition. Everything is reported if possible by messengers or eye-witnesses ; in Act II, scene 5, Hircan and the soldiers of the guard report that Holofernes has been led intoxicated into his tent, whither Judith has followed him ; in the next scene, Abra fills out with a prayer to God the space of time necessary for Judith's deed (apparently, at least, for there are no stage directions). She says :

> ' Sie will das Haupt abhauen,
> Das ich auch anzuschauen
> Zu furchtsam bin ' ;

---

1. This source is now known to be Andrea Salvadori's *Giuditta*, an opera with music by Marco da Gagliano performed in Florence in 1626. For a full discussion of Opitz's treatment of his source v. Anton Mayer: *Quelle und Entstehung von Opitzens Judith* in *Euphorion* XX (Leipzig und Wien 1913) pp. 39 ff. In general he may be said only to have altered details of the text.

and Judith immediately follows this by :

' Abra, nimm es hin... '

Similarly, in the third act, Bagos reports the fact of Holofernes' murder to Hircan.

The whole impression is indeed musical rather than dramatic ; one of the effective moments in Act III is that in which, following immediately on the lamentations of Bagos over the body of Holofernes, the cry of the Hebrews is heard afar off within the city ; and this is an essentially musical effect. Directly traceable to operatic influence also is the comparatively important rôle played by the soldiers of the guard, who exist chiefly in order to provide good choruses (as in II. 3) [1]. The course of events, compressed as it is bound to be into a small space, follows the main lines of the biblical narrative ; but the atmosphere is entirely altered, and a new element is introduced in the principal characters. The conception of Holofernes recalls that of Hudson's translation of Saluste du Bartas' *Historie of Judith* [2] (also of Romance origin) where the Assyrian is thus described :

'The courteous Gen' rall mildly gan her greet.
My love I am, I am not yet so fell
As false report doth to you Hebrews tell ',

and where he gives vent to his sorrows in these terms :

' I rage, I burn, I dye in desp'rate thought ',
Through love, by this same stranger's beauty brought. '

It was the fate of Opitz's opera to be expanded by one of its author's disciples. Andreas Tscherning, a Silesian poet, follower and friend of Opitz, conceived the idea of adding to the latter's play two introductory acts shewing the events leading up to the crisis with which Opitz had begun — *viz.* Judith's interview with Holofernes in the Assyrian camp. In this way he thought to bring Opitz's text into conformity with the regular five-act play, failing to grasp the musical operatic nature of the work he was attempting

---

1. In the songs of the Chorus Opitz seems to have been most independent of his model (v. A. Mayer : art. cit. p. 44) ; in them his partiality for mythology, learned names and allusions found full scope.

2. v. Chronological Survey, No 23.

to expand. His ideas were derived from the older ' Schuldrama ' ; Opitz, on the other hand, drew his inspiration from Italian opera. With two such different conceptions, no homogeneous work could be expected ; and in fact we find considerable discrepancies between the two parts of Tscherning's *Judith*, published in 1646. In the two acts added by Tscherning there is only one chorus; the author makes no attempt at imitating Opitz's variations of metre, and even the ' Opitzische Redensarten ' which, as he tells us in the Preface, he has been at pains to cultivate, do not help to remove the inconsistencies of characterisation and the difference of atmosphere. Even within Tscherning's two additional acts, certain inconsistencies may be detected— Pagao, for instance, is at one time peaceful, at another warlike ; Ozias is now self-reliant, now irresolute. The reviser only adds incidents already familiar in the older Judith dramas. He keeps closely to the original story, and only in the descriptions of the distress prevailing in Bethulia does experience of reality impart vividness to his writing [1]. Such in fact is his habitual dependence, in his other works, upon previous models, that the suggestion has been offered that he drew from some definite dramatic version even in writing the two preliminary acts which he adds to Opitz's opera. Dr. Borcherdt [2] finds many general resemblances between them and the Latin drama of Sixt Birck, though he admits differences of detail, and in order to account for these, he suggests that Tscherning may have used a ' watered-down version ', but is unable to offer any suggestion as to this version [3]. More striking parallels might be drawn between Tscherning's work and the *Judith* of Hans Sachs however [4]. But

---

1. Cp. Rose's *Holofern*, where the same statement may be made with reference to Rose's descriptions, even though the latter borrowed largely from Tscherning's version.

2. v. H. H. Borcherdt : *Andreas Tscherning*. München u. Leipzig, 1912. ch. XI, pp. 112 ff. and p. 291.

3. H. H. Borcherdt : *op. cit.* p. 112 and, p. 291.

4. The following table of parallel scenes may indicate the resemblances :

Hans Sachs	*Tscherning*
I. 1. Council of Nebucadnezar, where Pagoa, the ' Kriegsrath ', advises peace and Holofernes war.	I. 1. Council of Nebucadnezar, where Pagoa, the ' Kriegsrath ' advises peace and Holofernes war.
I. 2. Discourse on terrible deeds of Holofernes, between ' Ponto, der Mesopotamier ' and ' ein Cilicier '.	I. 2. Discourse about Holofernes among ' Nathan, ein Mesopotamier ', ' Agenor, ein Cilizier ', and ' Ponto ' ein Lybier '.

in any case, these acts add nothing new to the treatment of the story. They constitute Tscherning's only attempt at drama (though he wrote an oratorio on a biblical theme : *Von der Aufferweckung Lazari*) ; and he is on the whole justified in his own verdict : ' Mir ist nicht unbewust / dass zur Vollkommenheit eines Schauspiels ein mehres gehöre / als die Ohnmacht meines Verstandes kann fassen' [1].

The title of a third opera on Holofernes, by Joachim Beccau,— *L'Amor insanguinato*, published in 1720—is in itself a sufficient indication that this version marks a further stage of operatic development, in which Italian models have exerted a wholly

Carmi and Jojakim, the High Priest, pray to God for help, Osias orders the fortification of the town.	Prayer of Carmi and Jojakim. Osias orders the fortification of the town. A hymn to God ends the scene.
II. 1. Achior relates the history of the Hebrews and is bound to a tree by order of Holofernes.	I. 3. Achior relates the history of the Hebrews, and is sentenced by Holofernes. The episode is expanded (the improbable detail of Achior's monologue while hanging on the tree being added).
II. 2. Achior's account to Osias and the consequent consternation in Bethulia.	II. 1. Achior's account to Osias and the consequent consternation in Bethulia.
II. 3. Short dialogue between Holofernes and Pagoa.	II. 2. Conversation of Holofernes, Arsace and Hircan.
II. 4. Despair in Bethulia. The water supply has been cut off. The citizens pray the Elders to surrender ; Carmi advises a delay of 5 days.	II. 3. Despair in Bethulia.
	II. 4. Council of Holofernes decides to cut off the water supply from Bethulia.
	II. 5. Still greater despair in Bethulia. The citizens pray the Elders to surrender. Osias decides, on the advice of Jojakim, to wait 5 days.
II. 5. Judith enters, reproaches the Elders for their lack of courage and announces that she has a plan.	II. 6. Judith enters, reproaches the Elders for their lack of courage and announces that she has a plan.
III. 1. Judith's preparations. She prays for help. The Elders wish her well as she goes out.	II. 7. Judith prepares and prays for help.
	II. 8. (Am Tore) expands the comments of the Elders as Judith emerges.
III. 2. Judith arrives at the camp of Holofernes.	III. 1. Judith arrives at the camp of Holofernes. Here begins ' Herrn Opitzen Arbeit '.

1. v. H. H. Borcherdt : *op. cit.* p. 116.

pernicious influence. If more evidence were required, the list of dramatis personae would supply it. Achior ' liebet die Printzessin Japhite ' (a princess of Midian) ; Licor, a prince of Hyrcania, is ' Nebenbuhler des Achior und General Lieutenant des Holofernes ' ; and Judith herself is described as ' Eine galante Wittwe und Standesperson aus Bethulia '. Italian arias are inserted into the text, with a German prose translation printed in small type beside them (e. g. Act I, scene 2, ' se mio furore sfrenato lampeggia ') ; but we also find ' comic ' scenes, often in dialect, among the soldiers. In these, such spectacles are seen as that of Evil (who virtually corresponds to the clown) playing at ombre with his boon companions. The three couples, Achior and Japhite, Holofernes and Judith, Evil and Abra, are treated as of almost equal importance. The first and the last couple are married after Judith has killed Holofernes, but the course of their love does not run smoothly throughout ; Achior, in despair at his apparently unrequited passion, is prepared to commit suicide in the first act, but Japhite, strolling in the same direction for the purpose of confiding to the audience that she can no longer bear to conceal her feelings, appears at the right moment to save him. (Evil, however, who has serious thoughts of following suit in the matter of suicide, succeeds in persuading himself by reasoning, without Abra's aid, that the time is not yet come for such drastic measures). The Elders of Bethulia are in love with Judith for her beauty, and declare the fact in ' asides ' (e. g. in Act II, sc. 9) ; Bagoas, as well as his Chief, is tortured by her eyes, as are Zelot and Merit, two youths who meet her by chance. It is in fact the fashion to fall in love with the fair Jewess at sight ; but she, for her part, is troubled by no scruples when she cuts off Holofernes' head. Abra's comment sufficiently indicates the mind of her mistress :

' Dem ist die Courtoisie nur schlecht bekommen '.

Supernatural machinery is used throughout. Even as early as Act II, (sc. 1) we are left in no doubt as to the result, for a rift appears in the clouds, Jehovah is seen seated on a throne, encircled by fire, and angels sing an aria round Judith ;

' Durch eines Weibes Hand
Soll Holofernes fallen
So wird gewiss bey allen
Des Höchsten Ruhm bekandt. '

The charms of dance and ballet are freely used throughout the opera—a dance of satyrs and field-spirits closes the first act, one of ' Amourettes ' shooting golden arrows (to symbolise the meeting of Judith and Holofernes) ends the second act, and that of Evil with two little harlequins the third. Act IV ends with a dance of ghosts and night spirits after the murder of Holofernes, and a grand ballet after Act V concludes the whole. Unfortunately but little of the music of these 18th century operas has been preserved; but that it was ornate may be gathered from the libretto, and that the influence of Italy was paramount is evident from this treatment of even a biblical theme [1].

The alternative to an operatic setting of Scriptural subjects, in Germany as in England, was the oratorio. Here too the influence of the Jesuit drama and its imitators may be traced. Such a play as the Franciscan *Judith* of 1763 (Aachen, periocha) with its German arias (Canto solo, Basso solo in Act I, Duetto and Recitative in Act III, and the final ' tutti ' aria) is obviously a forerunner of the stricter oratorio, where the musical element becomes all-important. A record is found of a performance in 1704 at Vienna of such an oratorio [2]. In England in the 18th century two different settings were published. The first, in 1733, was *Judith*, ' an oratorio or sacred drama ' by W... H... Esq., the music to which was composed by William de la Fesch, late Chapel-Master of the Cathedral Church at Antwerp [3]. The second, dating from 1761, was a ' sacred drama with music by Dr. Arne ', and was performed at the Theatre Royal in Drury Lane, and again, three years later, at the Lock Hospital Chapel. In each case the music is obviously of more importance than the text, and the names of Arne and De Fesch guarantee a higher level in the former than is attained by the very mediocre

---

1. A considerable number of records of operatic versions & performances in the late 18th and 19th centuries exists — v. Chronological Survey Nos 75, 76, 89, 93. That the theme is still considered suitable for operatic treatment is evident from the fact. that the latest version to be chronicled is an opera. v. Chron. : Survey Nº 102 (note).

2. v. Chronological Survey No. 54. and supra, p. 77, note 2) where the performance in Vienna of two Italian oratorios on *Giuditta* is noted.

3. The frontispiece to this work in the British Museum copy is by Hogarth, with the quotation underneath : Per vulnera servor Morte tua vivens. *Virgil*. The work (which is by William Huggins) was performed ' with scenes and other decorations ', but met with no success. v. *Works of Hogarth* ed. J. Nicholson and G. Steevens, London, 1810. vol. II. p. 94. cp. also vol. II. p. 109, for a Hogarth print of a ' rehearsal of the oratorio of *Judith* '. (1808).

libretto.   In the latter there is little worthy of note ; the choruses and arias form by far the most important part of the three-act oratorio : the recitatives exist merely to shew the course of events. The language is that of the conventional love-poem of the day, and there is little difference between oratorio and opera in this respect. In the *Judith* of 1733, Holofernes addresses the heroine in gallant speeches and finally raises her to her feet with the words :

> ' ...Rise,
> My fair one, thou hast fail'd in thy Design,
> Thou cam'st to be my slave, but I am thine' (III, 1) ;

this is immediately followed by the air :

> ' The queen of beauty does ordain
> You over human Kind shall reign
> The Conqu'ror of all Hearts :
> Love does to your Eyes repair
> And furnishes his Quiver there
> With never-erring Darts.'

Holofernes is painted first as a gallant courtier, then as a burning lover, and finally—in grotesque and unsuitable fashion—as a drunken tyrant.   Judith is not an impressive figure, and her qualms of conscience are particularly ineffective :

> ' ...no weapon with me
> But my Fraud, forgive me Heav'n
> The Artifice I use,
> To save my poor distressèd Country.'   (II, 4).

Then in the aria to this she announces her intention of flattering and deceiving Holofernes. Bagoas is the typical confidential servant of 18th century drama ; he is ready at any moment to assist in the execution of his master's schemes, but when Holofernes is dead he exclaims :

> I'll fly where-ever
> My Despair transports me.   (runs off).   (III, 4).

The author felt it impossible to present the murder of Holofernes ; he therefore adopted the expedient (already practised in the popular plays) of giving stage directions that the head should be cut off behind the canopy of the bed.

The sacred drama of 1761 shares with the preceding oratorio
the characteristics of musical form and of 18th century language.
The airs and choruses are in lyric measures, the recitatives in blank
verse.   Holofernes thus announces Judith's approach :

> ' ...Fair Judith còmes,
> Another Venus by the Graces led.
> So when the Sea-born Goddess from the Foam
> Prolific sprung, as on the boiling Deep
> Her Form appear'd, the loud Winds fell to Whispers
> And the Waves crept in Murmurs to the Shore. '   (II, 7).

Similarly Abra, in consigning Holofernes to the care of Judith
in his tent, says :

> ' Bacchus to Venus has resign'd the Hero,
> With Wine oppressed...'   (II, 7).

But there is greater dignity in this version than in that of 1733.
Judith shews resolution and strength ; she keeps her plan concealed
from all ; and in her self-communing reveals a religious spirit
completely absent in the preceding oratorio :

> ' With some vast
> Design my Soul is big ! Yet what am I,
> Most Gracious ! What am I that thou shouldst do
> This Thing, and by an Instrument so feeble
> Blazon thy glorious Name among the Nations.'   (I, 4).

And this is immediately followed by the air :

> ' Adventurous, lo ! I spread the sail. '

Moreover, some skill is shewn in the structure of this musical
drama.   There is unity of treatment, even if the treatment be
slight.

The remaining musical version of the Judith theme in England is
in the form of a cantata written in 1858 for the Birmingham
Musical Festival.   But here there is no dramatic treatment in the
ordinary sense of the word ; the text, moreover, is entirely ' selected
from Holy Scriptures '.   Only the introductory remarks are of
interest, from their criticism of the theme, its reputation and
possibilities.   The author of the text (H. F. Chorley) contrasts
the ' moral of large application ' in the episodes of the Old and New

Testaments with the picturesque quality of the Apocryphal histories. Judith, in his view, belongs to ' the world of special tradition, not of universal instruction. This is a legend of the heroine who availed herself of her beauty to " answer a fool according to his folly "—who conceived herself empowered to deal subtly with a brutal invader " for the exaltation of Jerusalem " and for the deliverance of a beleaguered people. It is no lesson '. The subject, he adds, has often been handled for the foreign stage ' owing to the picturesque contrasts which it presents ', but has always of necessity been ' more or less objectionable ' [1].

It is interesting to note the appreciation of the story's dramatic possibilities in the author of an undramatic Cantata in Three Parts ; and interesting also to observe the criticism of such operatic versions as were commonly presented abroad.   On the whole, however, it seems justifiable to maintain that the predominantly musical versions of the theme add little of interest in the treatment of the story, though they undoubtedly added to its popularity, and though they contribute data for our consideration of the general mode of dealing with biblical subjects in the 17th and 18th centuries.

The early versions of the 19th century give little indication of the immense change which was to take place in the presentation of the tale (and character) of Judith towards the middle of the century, and to make of it a modern dramatic theme.   The *Judith* of Heinrich Keller of Zürich [2] in 1809 is a ' Romantic ' drama, purporting to be copied from a mediaeval MS. by ' Heinrich von Itzenloe, Hofpoet bey Kaiser Rudolf II '.   Written in rhymed strophes of five lines (rhyming on the pattern abaab, or sometimes abbab) it has, of necessity, more of a lyric and narrative than a dramatic character ; and the constraint of form reacts inevitably upon the characterisation.

The action of the play differs considerably from the original story.   Much is added in the way of episodes, but the principal change is a radical one ; love and gallantry are made the chief interest.   The whole intrigue is re-constructed from this point of view ; while retaining the main facts of Judith's widowhood, her

1. Yet, he adds, for the name of Judith's attendant (Amital) he is indebted to Metastasio's *Betulia liberata*.   His strictures therefore apply in all probability to Italian or French operatic treatments.

1. v. B. Wyss : *Heinrich Keller. Der Züricher Bildhauer und Dichter*.   Frauenfeld, 1891, pp. 49 ff.

beauty, and her mode of achieving deliverance for Bethulia, the author creates an atmosphere different from that of almost all the purely dramatic versions (apart from operas and oratorios) in Germany and England. Countless combats take place in Bethulia between Judith's rival suitors ; Eliab loves her passionately, until in the end act she hands him over to her favourite, Recha. Eliab acquiesces, regarding Judith as something of a goddess ; and there ensue long scenes of love-rapture which are apart from the main action. Holofernes himself is utterly unlike a tyrant and despot in his intercourse with Judith [1].

> ' Darf ich glauben dem Entzücken ? ' he cries ;
> Diesen Schnee und diese Rosen
> Soll ich an den Busen drücken,
> Soll mit sanften Blumen kosen
> Und in Sternenaugen blicken ? '

The figure of Holofernes, the courtier-lover, is comparatively uninteresting, however, beside that of Judith. Her keenness of wit and decision of character make of her a redoubtable adversary. At the banquet in the third act she completely deceives Holofernes by her flattering love-speeches ; yet she is not wholly without qualms of conscience. She prays to be forgiven for stooping to feminine wiles to overthrow the enemy :

> ' Heut sey ich nicht um meine Schuld gerichtet :
> Es werde nicht dein Israel durch mich,
> Die schmerzlich reu'ge Sünderin, vernichtet.'

She exhorts Delia (the Abra of the apocryphal story) to courage until after the deed is done ; then, while she hastens away, she confesses to fear : ' Ein Schauder fasst mich '. Her bitter complaint at the universal judgment : ' Weiber haben keine Thaten ' is an expression of one of the strongest traits in her character. Her soul revolts against the submission to men's judgment and men's love that is expected of her as a woman ; she is of a proud heart and fiery temper.

> ' Schwach ist der Männer Streben, wie ihr Wollen ;
> Leicht wandelbar verwerfen sie und wählen :
> Ein weiblich Herz kann wahre Kraft nur stählen ;'

---

1. His gallantry is such that Jacob Grimm comments that this trait, as well as the verse-form, must have been due to the influence of Spanish drama. (Review of Heinrich von Itzenloe : *Judith*, in J. Grimm : *Kleinere Schriften* vol. VI (Rezensionen und Vermischte Aufsätze III. Theil) Berlin 1882, p. 11).

she says ; and again :

> ' Kein Mann regt sich für Juda als Befreyer ;
> Ein kühnes Weib wird den Triumph erjagen — '

a sentence outlining one of the motives of Hebbel's Judith. In her previous marriage she was bound against her will ; now, she says, she is

> ' Jetzt befreyt — nur wo ich morden
> Wollte, könnt' ich Liebe heucheln — '

—a sinister and interesting prediction. A sentence in one of Keller's letters throws light on this aspect of Judith's character : ' Nun habe ich ein Stück zu Ehren der Frauen geschrieben ; unzufrieden mit der elenden Darstellung weiblicher Wesen in Romanen und Komödien, wollt ' ich die Ehre der Frauen verfechten, da ich so viele der vortrefflichsten ihres Geschlechtes kannte ' [1]. There is little doubt that we can detect in this play also the influence of contemporary conditions. The women of the ' Romantic school ' had already challenged the prevailing ideas of woman's sphere and mission, of the restraints and conventions to which she should be subject. It is appropriate that in *Judith*, a ' Romantic drama ', Keller should break a lance in the cause of women's emancipation.

A complete contrast to this attitude, and a curious manifestation of reaction against the popular view of Judith's act, is to be found in a drama, *Judith und Holofernes*, published at Zerbst in 1818. In the Preface to this singular production, the anonymous author explains that the drama has no general anti-Semitic bias, but is intended to express detestation of Judith's deed ' die den tiefsten Abscheu in jedem rechtschaffenen Herzen erregende Missethat der schönen Judith, in so fern diese die Alles, was da lebt, beglückende heilige Liebe missbrauchte, um einen grossen edelmüthigen Feldherrn meuchlerisch zu ermorden, und wovon die Geschichte nicht in einem kanonischen Buche der Bibel, sondern bloss in einem apokryphischen, geschrieben stehet, folglich gedachter unerhörte Meuchelmord nicht von Jehovah selbst befohlen worden ist, immerdar fort als eine löbliche That gerühmt, und nie in ihrer gottesläst-erlichen Blösse dargestellt worden... ' (p. 7). The rôle of Achior is here merged in that of the Tempter ; Adramelech (Satan's prime

---

1. v. B. Wyss : *op. cit.* p. 50 and note on p. 69.

minister), Uriel, a ' Jewish seraph ', and Achior ' represent one
and the same person ' (according to a note appended to the list
of dramatis personae) ; this character, it is stated, can never dis-
card the cloven hoof, but conceals it as much as possible.   Throughout, Achior and the seraph inspire the actions of the Jews, and in
particular those of Judith.   There is not even an element of dramatic surprise in this, for Adramelech appears in the opening
scene, in the guise of Achior, and explains, in hexameters, how he
has forsaken Holofernes for the Jews in order to confound the former
more effectually.   Hexameters alternate with verbose speeches in
prose through the whole play; the prevailing 'journalese' is only
relieved by dialect (e. g. in II. 1, where Achior, on the tree, cries
out in Yiddish-German and is answered in dialect by the Bethulians
who rescue him).   Adramelech appears when conjured up by the
cabbalistic magic of Charmi (II. 6), and accepts the latter's suggestion of Judith's action as better than the Satanic plans ; in the first
scene of Act III he then appears to Judith in her sleep, and in the
guise of Uriel suggests the plan to her.   On waking, she resolves
to carry it out : ' Ich—zwar nur ein schwaches, aber doch schönes
Weib, will allein das grosse, von Männern nicht zu überwindende
Heer des Nobuchadnosar mit einem einzigen Schwerdtstreich zu
nichte machen '.   The plan is prepared and carried out in the
traditional manner ; Holofernes is depicted as a gentle tyrant, an
' edelmüthiger Feldherr ' in the scene where he and Judith meet
(III. 5).   The most significant and interesting point in the whole
drama occurs in this same scene : Abra relates the story of Judith
to Holofernes, and tells him that the illness of the former's husband
caused her marriage to be no real marriage : ' Dorüm hahst se nü
ane Wittib, is ober nür noch a Madje, as ech bin ahch '.   In view
of Hebbel's subsequent treatment, this idea is of great interest,
although there is no absolute evidence to prove that Hebbel knew
the anonymous play [1].   The fourth act shews the usual escape
and triumphant return of Judith, the discovery of Holofernes '
death by Poe (=Bagoa) : ' Komm nich !   Komm kann nich !
Kopp ab !   Kopp ab ! ', the flight of the Assyrians, and the greed
of the Jews in acquiring plunder.   The last act brings the solution
of the Achior problem.   Judith confides to Hosias the identity

---

1. There is no suggestion of the idea in the apocryphal book, nor in any of the versions extant before 1818.   Cp. however Hebbel's discussion of the point in his
diary. v. infra, pp. 97-98.

of Achior and the seraph of her dream (which has been revealed
to her), and Hosias suggests to Achior that he should marry Judith.
A love scene between them is succeeded by a betrothal scene ;
immediately afterwards Adramelech reveals himself to her, and
drags her with him as he sinks to hell in a storm of thunder and
lightning.

It is clear that the play has no real dramatic value, and even the
simple course of events is spoilt by the attempt at satire and propaganda.   But the incidental picture of Judith is of historical interest
in the light of later dramas ; while the dialect portions seem to be
descended from the older form of ' Volksschauspiel '.

In *The Fair Avenger* or *The Destroyer destroyed*, written in 1825
by J. F. Pennie and specifically called an ' academic drama ', the
didactic motive of the scholastic plays and the rhetoric of opera
libretto are combined.   The work is of little value ; but at least
the author's Preface does not encourage expectations.   He maintains the superiority of Scriptural subjects, and mentions that many
conductors of ' respectable Seminaries for youth ' are often at a
loss for a suitable and harmless drama.   As ' a strictly moral piece '
none, he says, can object to *The Fair Avenger*, while ' that laudable
patriotism, so strikingly displayed in the history of Judith, renders
it peculiarly fitted for scholastic representation '.   It is, he points
out, conveniently short for such a purpose.   Here is an echo of
the didacticism of the earlier plays on Judith ;   while there is a
distinct suggestion of the operatic hero in Holofernes :

' Transcendent fair one, from thy lips do flow
The words of wisdom, like the honey-dews
Dropping from morning roses...
...In Nineve's gold-bannered halls of state
Shalt thou, the peerless queen of love and beauty
And this adoring heart, supremely reign.'   (III, 2).

In the same vein is the stage direction that boys dressed in white,
bearing incense and flowers, should strew these in Judith's path—
this in the tent of war of a fierce Assyrian chieftain.   The one
episode invented by the author is similar in character.   Arbona
and Sanbassarus, two captains in Holofernes' army, are sharply
differentiated in the first act by their desire for wealth and fame
respectively.   Arbona conceives the idea of carrying Judith off
to his desert home, and lies in wait for her when she and her maid

Thirza go outside the camp to pray.   Judith is about to rouse the guards by cries for protection, when Sanbassarus appears ; he challenges and kills Arbona.   During the combat Judith, to the chagrin of Sanbassarus, escapes back to her tent.   Such an episode of a minor love interest resembles the additions in many of the 18th century treatments.   In a similar spirit, the question of scenic representation of the death of Holofernes is solved by making Thirza, who stands outside the tent, hear and describe the sounds which indicate what is happening within.   The familiar device of a dramatic report is unskilfully used, however, and the scene verges on the ludicrous.

The chief virtue of the drama is its brevity — already emphasised by the author in its preface.   Each of the first two acts consists of one long scene : the grand council of Holofernes, ending with the banishment of Achior, and the revolt in Bethulia, where Ozias yields to the citizens and Judith reproaches him and heartens the despairing crowd in a prophetic speech.   Her first entry has some grandeur, and the speech of Ozias reflects the general recognition of this :

> ' O what a brow of majesty she wears. '   (II, 1).

(the effect is not improved however by the addition of :

> ' And what rich light breaks from her heaven-blue eye,
>   Illuming the soft beauty of her cheek ! ')

There is a definite attempt to make her an impressive and inspired figure, and her great speech to the crowd partially succeeds in accomplishing this, though it errs on the side of rhetoric :

> ' Ask not of me the act that I shall do,
> For I will not declare it. O, I feel
> Prophetic inspiration on me rush,
> And an heroic spirit lifting me
> To more than mortal deeds.   Darkness and storms
> Have hung on Zion's towers, but glory soon
> Shall in full splendour o'er the temple burst,
> I see the angel of the host of heaven
> Clad in the glories of the midday sun !
> His flaming sword shall guard me.—On to victory !'   (II, 1).

This is however the only occasion on which the work rises to anything like poetic quality ; and it is as much a lyrical as a dramatic occasion. The end is unexpectedly brief; battle, victory, song of triumph and procession are omitted, and the drama ends with a speech of Judith, in which she advises the Bethulians to attack the enemy at break of day. Possibly the difficulty of representing a battle with the dramatic resources of most ' seminaries ' restrained the author from attempting to pourtray the flight of the Assyrians and the rejoicing in Bethulia which form the natural ending to the story.

It is not easy to include this treatment in any definite category. Least of all is it characteristic of the drama of the 19th century ; it still breathes the atmosphere of a didactic exercise and an 18th century ' Singspiel '.

That the fashion of musical settings for the tale of Judith and Holofernes continued to be popular in the early 19th century is suggested by one of the ' Phantasiestücke ' of Carl Weisflog, published in 1824 : *Der wüthende Holofernes*. This little prose sketch purports to be an account of an oratorio performed to celebrate a ducal birthday : ' Bericht des Hof-Cantoris Hilarius Grundmaus A. D. 1616. Ans Licht gestellet von mir und gedruckt in diesem Jahr '. The music is the work of the Hof-Cantor himself ; the text is by ' Matthäus Pflaumenkern' and the title ' ein geistliches Oratorium, betitelt : der wüthende, aber mit Gottes Hülfe dennoch besiegte Holofernes, oder das befreiete Bethulia '. A description of the performance follows, in an attractive vein of humorous parody ; and it is highly probable that it notes most of the salient points of such representations. The work is supposed to be in three parts : no fewer than 576 instrumentalists and 919 singers take part (including, no doubt significantly, an Italian fiddler). First is shewn the march of the Assyrians ; Holofernes in a recitative curses the Jews, who answer him in a chorus and are themselves answered again by the Assyrians. Achior's narrative, exile and ' Lamentoso ' conclude the first part. In the second, Judith and Abro (*sic*) sing a duet expressing hope and faith. Choruses and soli follow, among the Jews. Judith decides on Achior's release, and the farewell aria is played by the violinist, ' largo grazioso ' with his fiddle behind his back. In the next part, Judith and Abro are among the Assyrian soldiers. ' Allerlei Kurzweil ' takes place, and at the ensuing banquet of Holofernes, birthday greetings are presented to the Churfürst in whose honour the performance is being held. Judith wins over Holofernes and remains behind with him during

the playing of a ' nocturne '.　She cuts off his head ; the head
immediately sings a pathetic aria beginning :

> ' Verruchte Hand, die mir
> das Lebenslicht geraubt. '

Judith and Abro bear back the head in triumph.　A chorus greets
them, including the march of the Jews, the lament and flight of
the Assyrians.　The work ends with a double fugue.

The little sketch is in the manner of E. T. Hoffmann and has
something of his charm.　The most obvious points of the parody
are sufficiently illuminated by a survey of the versions of the Judith
story current in the 18th century—the absurdities of the birthday
greetings and the aria sung by the head, the pretentious character
of the opening and concluding scenes with their lack of any sem-
blance of probability, can at once be parallelled in such treatments
as *L'Amor insanguinato* (1720), while records of operas (and a
' melodrama') in 1732, 1798, 1799 shew that the continued popularity of the type gave ground for parody.

It is one of the most abrupt transitions in the varied history of
the tale of Judith when we turn from Weisflog's burlesque sketch
to the treatment which chronologically succeeds it — the *Judith*
of Friedrich Hebbel (1840).　Here, the characters seem to move
in a different world.　The theme is outwardly the same, the
subject of the eighty-three versions which precede this drama ;
but inwardly it has been metamorphosed.　Not only is the dramatic
conflict inherent in the story sharpened and lifted to the height
of a tragic opposition.　The conflict itself is no longer solely one
of individuals : it has become a fundamental antagonism of God
against Gods, of Judaism against paganism, of sex against sex, of
the individual against the world-necessity.　That is to say, the
story, in the process of dramatisation, has become for the dramatist
the symbolical representation of the forces which, in his vision,
conflict in the world of man and ultimately condition human
existence.　At last, after surviving for varying reasons, after
adapting itself to changing conditions, the story has become
universalised.　It has at the same time, by a familiar paradox,
become more individual, in that both Judith and Holofernes are
intensely individual figures.　For Hebbel, just as much as for the
authors of *Victrix fiducia Bethuliae* or *Judith... Exemplum reipublicae recte institutae,* Judith represents an idea.　But she represents

it because of and through her individual character ; she does not
exist to exemplify the idea.   From being a subject for didactic
drama she has beccme a subject for psychological drama—a tragic
heroine.   She is not only concerned with an outward battle, against
the enemy of her people ; she is disturbed by an inner conflict of
motive in herself.   She is no longer only a channel for the divine
purposes ; she is an individual woman, whose instincts, if not her
will, assert themselves against her mission.   Only by means of
the realisation and pourtrayal of such an inner conflict can the
Judith of the Apocrypha become the central figure of a tragedy.
The only faint foreshadowing of this, before Hebbel's drama, is in
the Preface to Opitz's opera, and in Keller's *Judith*.   In both these,
however, fraud is excused by motive—in the one case on religious,
in the other on feminist grounds.   Hebbel, on the other hand, does
not seek to excuse or to defend Judith's action in deceiving Holofernes ; he analyses her real motives, and shews the crucial change
in them when she comes into contact with a spirit even stronger
than her own.   Thus her inward conflict arises, and only thus does
she become a tragic figure.

Although *Judith* is Hebbel's first drama, it reveals with singular
clarity the main ideas which characterise his later work.   The
world, as Hebbel perceives it, is a world of tragic contradiction ;
the individual will conflicts inevitably with the world-will—
represented, in *Judith*, by the will of God.   An omnipotent God
requires utter submission from his creatures, who yet can only
carry out His will by developing and acting for themselves.
God can only use as His instrument the human being who has
become individualised, and therefore free ; but God himself is
powerless to save this individual from destruction in the process
of obedience.   Similarly, the individual can only fulfil his destiny,
fully become himself, by insurrection, assertion of his individual
right ; yet this same assertion must inevitably be crushed by the
universal force—the world-will, or idea.   ' Das Leben ist der
grosse Strom, die Individualitäten sind Tropfen, die tragischen aber
Eisstücke, die wieder zerschmolzen werden müssen und sich, damit
dies möglich sey, an einander abreissen und zerstossen '[1].   Strength
alone is of value in life, and strength brings its own destruction.

This idea of an essential dualism in life is the fundamental

---

1. Tagebuch. Copenhagen, March 6. 1843. in *Tagebücher* herausgeg. R. M. Werner.
Berlin-Steglitz. (N. D.) vol. II. (1840-44) p. 239.

assumption of Hebbel's drama. ' Menschennatur ' is opposed to
' Menschengeschick ' ; it is the problem of drama to solve the
contradiction [1]. That which is tragic is the actual conflict in a man,
not the result of that conflict. It is not so much the fact of guilt
in any given human being as the necessity of guilt implied in the
very nature of his freedom and development, that makes life, in
its essence, material for tragedy. Good conflicts with good, not
good with evil, in the deepest tragic opposition. Every tragic
figure must contain the elements of greatness ; herein lies the
compensation—the solution of the riddle, in so far as solution is
offered. Action and development make life worth living, even
though in their complete fulfilment they necessitate the surrender
of man, as individual, to the infinitely more powerful force of the
' world-will '—or universal law.

The figures of Judith and Holofernes illustrate this conception.
Their tragedy is set against a large historical background ; in their
conflict is mirrored the battle of Israel against heathendom [2].
Holofernes disturbs the cosmic harmony by the violent assertion
of Titanic strength; Judith, divinely appointed as the instrument
to set this upheaval right, generates another in the process. She
steps outside the boundaries of her womanhood ; she becomes
thereby an individual transgressing the limits set to individual
action, and she too pays toll. Had she been able to carry out her
mission of killing Holofernes merely as a channel of the divine will,
she would have incurred no tragic guilt—this was the Judith of the
Apocrypha. But, in Hebbel's view, it is impossible for any woman
to accomplish such a deed impersonally. By an inevitable confusion
of motive, she herself takes part in the action and thereby becomes
subject to the tragic law of retribution for her self-assertion. The
Apocryphal Judith Hebbel regards with horror as ' eine Charlotte
Corday ' [3], ' eine Wittwe, die den Holofernes durch List und
Schlauheit ins Netz lockt—... Das ist gemein ; eine solche Natur
ist ihres Erfolgs gar nicht würdig ' [4]. Gradually her character

---

1.. *Tagebücher*, ed. cit. March 10, 1838, vol. I, p. 223.

2. v. *Tagebücher*, ed. cit. vol. II, p. 26, in a letter of April 3. 1840 to Frau Stich-
Crelinger, where Hebbel elaborates this statement.

3. *Mein Wort über das Drama* in *Sämtliche Werke* ed. R. M. Werner. vol. XI, p. 14.
Berlin, 1904.

4. *Tagebücher* ed. cit. Jan. 3. 1840. vol. II, p. 2. It is interesting to note how
Hebbel's conception, as often, arises out of a critical analysis of previous pourtrayals
of the character. This is characteristic of his mind and may be noted especially

unfolds itself to him ; from Oct. 3rd, 1839 (when he first announces in his diary that *Judith* is begun) entries succeed each other irregularly, shewing the ideas which occur to him as he writes. An important point arises on October 28th : ' Die Motive vor einer That verwandeln sich meistens während der That und scheinen wenigstens nach der That ganz anders : dies ist ein wichtiger Umstand, den die meisten Dramatiker übersehen ' [1]. Judith is representative of her sex, and her act is characteristic : ' In der Judith zeichne ich die *That* eines *Weibes*, also den ärgsten Contrast, dies Wollen und Nicht = Können, dies Thun, was doch kein Handeln ist ' [2]. She is thus opposed to the ' Handeln ' or creative act, of Holofernes—this is one of a group of smaller contrasts which form part of and enhance the basic conflict. A light is thrown on the inner destruction of Judith's personality by the entry : ' Der Geist soll den Körper durch den Gedanken vernichten, der Mensch, der stirbt *durch den blossen Gedanken, zu sterben*, hat seine Selbstbefreiung vollendet ' [3]. A long entry on January 3rd, 1840, discusses the difficulty (the ' innere Verlegenheit ') which Hebbel came to feel in the biblical Judith. The Judith of his drama is paralysed by her own act ; she is horrorstruck at the possibility of bearing a son to Holofernes, and realises at that moment that she has transgressed the conditions of her mission, ' dass sie über die Gränzen hinaus gegangen ist, dass sie mindestens das Rechte aus unrechten Gründen gethan hat ' [4]. This is the central point of the conflict in her ; but the difficulty in the dramatist's mind is the motivisation of her initial resolve. She cannot, Hebbel contends, be a widow, as in the biblical original—or her courage would not be equal to the decision. Nor can she be a maiden, whose sole source of strength would be lost in the confusion of experience. Thus the situation arises which is, (apart from the anonymous drama of 1818) Hebbel's peculiar addition to the story—she is ' zwischen Weib und Jungfrau in die Mitte gestellt ' and thereby is placed outside the limitations of

---

in his treatment of women e. g. Genoveva and Mariamne, Agnes Bernauer and Kriemhild.

1. *Tagebücher*, ed. cit. vol. I, p. 393.

2. *Tagebücher*, 24 Nov. 1839, ed. cit. vol. I, p. 404.

3. *Tagebücher*, 27 Dec. 1839. ed. cit. vol. I, p. 418. It is of interest to note that on Dec. 30, on receipt of a letter from Berlin asking for the MS of *Judith*, Hebbel expresses his distrust of ' das Theatralische ' and his conviction that the drama is unsuitable for stage representation. ' Die Poesie will ich wohl vertreten, aber das Theatralische macht mir grosse Sorgen '. vol. I, p. 421.

4. *Tagebücher*, ed. cit. vol. II, p. 2.

wifehood and maidenhood, and—we may add—in a psychological
state which has a considerable bearing both on her action itself and
on the confusion of her motives [1]. She is a finely-strung nature,
placed in a situation of peculiar complexity owing to the mysterious
circumstances of her marriage with Manasses.   She is only capable
of an act of murder under the stress of personal indignation ; thus
she discovers with horror that she has killed Holofernes in an impulse
of anger, not as a submissive instrument of God's purposes, but as
a woman avenging her individuality.   It is only by means of the
final situation, when Judith leaves her fate in the hands of God,
and exacts a promise from the Elders to kill her if she should require
it of them, that she can refrain from putting an end to her own life ;
inwardly indeed, we feel she is already dead : ' the spirit ' has
destroyed ' the body by an idea '.   She has asserted herself ; her
own personality has responded to, and then rebelled against, the
personality of Holofernes.   Her act of obedience becomes inevitably,
after the night in Holofernes' tent, an act of self defence : it is
changed from religious obedience to individual guilt.   Judith
realises, in response to Mirza's cry : ' Das also war's nicht, was
Dich trieb, als Du Deine Hand in Blut tauchtest ! ' that she has
betrayed her mission.   ' Aber jetzt muss ich meine That allein
tragen, und sie zermalmt mich ! '

If Judith represents the central problem of the drama, Holofernes
is nevertheless a more tragic figure than in any of the previous
versions of the story.   He personifies strength, without a restrain-
ing ethical force ; he rebels against all law outside himself.   Hence
the Israelites, trusting in a divine law, are essentially, as well as
by circumstance, antagonists ; he is resolved to shew that authority,
both human and divine, is powerless against his own forceful personality.   ' Hätt ' ich doch nur einen Feind, nur Einen, der mir
gegenüber zu treten wagte !   ich wollt' ihn küssen, ich wollte, wenn
ich ihn nach heissem Kampf in den Staub geworfen hätte, mich auf
ihn stürzen und mit ihm sterben !'   he cries in the first scene, which
is devoted to the exposition of his will to power.   Nebucad Nezar
he regards as a contemptible cipher, who has himself proclaimed
as a god and leaves the proof of his godhead to another : ' die
Menschheit hat nur den *einen* grossen Zweck, einen Gott aus sich
zu gebären ; und der Gott, den sie gebiert, wie will er zeigen, dass

---

1. v. also *Tagebücher*, ed. cit. vol. II, p. 19, where Hebbel discusses this point
in a letter to Frau Stich-Crelinger of March 7. 1840.

er's ist, als dadurch, dass er ihr zum ewigen Kampf gegenüber stellt, dass er all die thörichten Regungen des Mitleids, des Schauderns vor sich selbst, des Zurückschwindelns vor seiner ungeheuren Aufgabe unterdrückt, dass er sie zu Staub zermalmt, und ihr noch in der Todesstunde den Jubelruf abzwingt ? ' (I, 1).

The momentary thought that Judith may be deceiving him he at once rejects : ' Weib, es kommt mir vor, als ob Du mit mir spieltest. Doch nein, ich beleidige mich selbst, indem ich dies für möglich halte ' (IV, 1). Therefore Judith is able to tell him that she detests him, and that»she is come to murder him. Holofernes realises that the first statement is not wholly true and is thereby led to believe that the second is made in order to make the deed impossible.

He will accept no idea that is not his own ; when Judith in glowing words paints his triumph if he set the Hebrews free, that they might for ever be his slaves, he cries : ' Weib, ahnst Du auch, dass Du mir dies Alles unmöglich machst, indem Du mich dazu aufforderst ? Wäre der Gedanke in mir selbst aufgestiegen, vielleicht hätt' ich ihn ausgeführt. Nun ist er Dein und kann nimmer mein werden '. The gigantic strength of Holofernes is wonderfully conceived ; he is a mighty exaggeration, an isolated figure of paganism opposed to Israel's God. ' Was ist Sünde ? ' he asks, in childlike egotism. And on the other hand, the cry echoes in the streets of Bethulia : ' Heiliget Euch ! Heiliget Euch !' Who shall say where the victory lies ? Holofernes, despiser of all men for their weakness, dies by the hand of a woman he disdains to mistrust ; the inscrutable despot who cannot believe in doom or defeat, pays with life for his passion, which overleaps circumstance, religion and patriotism. But Judith also dies—in a real sense. Her personality is destroyed ; her independence is forfeit to a passion which her whole mind rejected, but which proved too potent for her spirit ; the very fate of her body is left undecided, is to be controlled by circumstance. The pride of her womanhood, the confidence of her religion, the inspiration of her patriotism, have been surrendered as the price of her combat with Holofernes ; she is no longer a sentient, active individual. Bethulia alone is the victor—the God of Israel has conquered paganism.

If the central idea of the story of is thus transformed by Hebbel, the treatment differs no less strikingly from that in the majority of earlier *Judith* dramas. Act I gives with wonderful conciseness the picture of Holofernes in the Assyrian camp. It is almost entirely occupied with the character of Holofernes, as shewn in his relations with soldiers and officers ; it only furthers the action by making known to us his resolve to destroy the Hebrews for being the last people to surrender to him and for daring to resist him. Act II gives a similar survey of the situation in Bethulia. Not the streets of the city (as in most versions) but Judith's apartment is chosen as the scene. Thus at once she enters into the same relations with Bethulia as does Holofernes with the camp. The latter has, of set purpose, made himself an unaccountable mystery : ' Das ist die Kunst, sich nicht auslernen lassen, ewig ein Geheimniss zu bleiben ! ' Judith is an enigma to herself ; she broods over the inscrutable mystery of her marriage with Manasses. She confides to Mirza the story of the vision which appeared to Manasses on their wedding night, and the secret of which died with him six months later. By this brooding she prepares the way for her sudden resolve in Act III. Meanwhile, to add to her motives, Ephraim comes to declare his love for her. She tests the strength of his passion, bidding him kill Holofernes, the enemy of Bethulia, if he would obtain her hand. He is afraid, however, to attempt the impossible, and the act closes on the words—significant for the processes of Judith's mind : ' Sehen alle Männer in der Gefahr Nichts, als die Warnung, sie zu vermeiden—dann hat ein Weib das Recht erlangt auf eine grosse That, dann—ha, ich hab' sie von Dir gefordert, ich muss beweisen, dass sie möglich ist ! ' A subtle trait of sex is here indicated ; Hebbel, as we know from the Tagebücher, meant Judith to represent ' dies Thun, was doch kein Handeln ist ', and her impulse here is based on a desire for action which is to carry her outside her sphere and spiritual capacities. This view is confirmed by Mirza's protest at the crucial moment in the action : ' Ein Weib soll Männer gebären ; nimmermehr soll sie Männer tödten ' (v, 1).

The third act opens with the scene of Judith's resolve. She has sat motionless, fasting, silent, and apparently hearing nothing, for three days and nights. Her prayer shews utter despair ; she has been filled with the idea of saving Bethulia by winning her way to Holofernes, but the way has not been revealed. ' In mir und ausser mir bleibt's dunkel'. Only one thought has come to her : ' Doch der kam nicht von Dir ! Oder kam er von Dir ?—(Sie springt auf) Er kam von Dir ! Der Weg zu meiner That geht durch die Sünde !... Vor Dir wird das Unreine rein ; wenn Du zwischen

mich und meine That eine Sünde stellst : wer bin ich, dass ich mit
Dir darüber hadern, dass ich mich Dir entziehen sollte ! ...Du
machtest mich schön ; jetzt weiss ich, wozu... '. This is the pure
logic of the visionary ; her resolve is taken, and she bids Mirza
adorn her, for ' Meine Schönheit ist jetzt meine Pflicht ! '

The scene changes to the streets of Bethulia, once Judith's decision
is taken ; a great crowd-scene follows, almost Shakespearean in
breadth and power. First the growing discontent among the
citizens bodes evil ; then the figure of the old, blind Samuel,
driven by his conscience to accuse himself of sin yet unrevealed,
passes across the stage. He is followed by Assad, counselling
surrender, who is suddenly condemned by his blind and dumb
brother Daniel, who breaks silence to prophesy and accuse : ' Steiniget ihn, steiniget ihn ! ' Only the misery of the populace is needed
to confirm Judith's resolution, and she leaves Bethulia, with Mirza,
for the camp of Holofernes.

Acts II and III thus give exposition and preparation leading
up to Judith's resolve : Acts IV and V give a parallel exposition and
preparation leading up to her action. Act IV is wholly taken up
with the meeting of Judith and Holofernes, where the former
succeeds in deceiving even Mirza as to her real object. The clash
of the two personalities is sufficient exposition for the tragedy of
the fifth act. Here the first scene shews us the final conflict of
strength between Judith and Holofernes—that is to say, the battle
in Judith's own soul. Her inner need of and longing for something
to be called a man compel her to admiration of his strength and
attract her to him against her reason and resolve. ' Gott meiner
Väter', she prays, ' schütze mich vor mir selbst, dass ich nicht
verehren muss, was ich verabscheue ! Er ist ein Mann' : and
' Hör' auf, hör' auf ! Ich muss ihn morden, wenn ich nicht vor
ihm knieen soll '. The inner confusion of motive has begun. She
feels him between her and her God : ' Ich muss beten in diesem
Augenblick, und kann's nicht ! ' Holofernes immediately replies :
' Stürz ' hin und bete mich an !'—and Judith recovers herself
for a moment : ' Dich ? Du trotzest auf Deine Kraft '. Driven
by an impulse she cannot explain or suppress, she tells him she
intends to murder him ; Holofernes, seeing in this but another
proof of his ascendancy, laughs her warning to scorn and drags
her into his tent.

Mirza remains in the outer tent, trembling and unnerved, divining the conflict behind the scenes. ' Dort wird Jemand ermordet ; ich weiss nicht, ob Holofernes oder Judith... ' Judith emerges, over-whelmed and unstrung, and by the narrative she pours into Mirza's ears rouses herself to vengeance on Holofernes as he sleeps. The sword is a gleaming hope : ' und hab ' ich in meiner Entwürdigung das Recht des Daseins eingebüsst : mit diesem Schwert will ich's mir wieder erkämpfen '. Hebbel makes it quite clear that the decisive motive of her act is vengeance. In the first moment of reaction, she almost kills herself, but Mirza hinders her. Never-theless Mirza's judgment is clear. She asks Judith why she came to the Assyrian camp : ' Hättest Du es nie betreten, Du hättest Nichts zu rächen gehabt '. Because of the misery of her people, Judith answers ; and this gives her confidence again : ' O, nun bin ich wieder mit mir ausgesöhnt. Dies Alles hatt ' ich über mich selbst vergessen ! ' But Mirza's pitiless logic sees the flaw in the argument : ' Du hattest es vergessen. Das also war's nicht, was Dich trieb, als Du Deine Hand in Blut tauchtest '.

Judith (langsam, vernichtet) 'Nein,—nein,—Du hast Recht, —das war's nicht,—Nichts trieb mich, als der Gedanke an mich selbst. O, hier ist ein Wirbel !... ' She prays for madness, but ' es dämmert nur hin und wieder ein wenig in mir, finster wird's nicht '. They set out for Bethulia, and Judith realises that praise and congratulation on her heroism will be her terrible reward.

The scene changes again to Bethulia at dawn on the fifth day, when the people are in utter misery. Judith and Mirza arrive and are greeted with praise and rejoicing ; but Judith is revolted by the clamour of the people against the Assyrians : ' Das ist Schläch-ter-Muth ! ' Priests and Elders urge her to demand her reward At first she indignantly refuses ; but a sudden thought comes to her, and after making them swear a solemn oath to fulfil her petition, she asks them to kill her if she should require this service of them. Only to Mirza does she explain her request : ' Ich will dem Holo-fernes keinen Sohn gebären. Bete zu Gott, dass mein Schooss unfruchtbar sei ! Vielleicht ist er mir gnädig ! ' In thus leaving her fate in the hands of God, Judith regains her sense of being an instrument of His purposes ; but the tragic catastrophe has already taken place. She can never regain her human happiness and freedom ; her only real life henceforth will be in the memory of her people.

There are two parallel actions in the drama : the outward, political and religious conflict between Hebrews and Assyrians, and the inward psychological conflict of act (representing human freedom) and circumstance (representing necessity—the world-will). Judith and Holofernes link both these actions together, and provide at the same time a number of smaller contrasts which enhance the main conflict. The structure of the play is saved from dualism by this insistent emphasis on one single point—the clash and interplay of the two chief personalities. This, together with the characteristic brevity of the drama, makes it extraordinarily forceful — an impression heightened by the vigorous, intense prose of the dialogue.

Criticism has not overlooked the obvious weaknesses of Hebbel's first play, whose merits have frequently been declared to lie rather in technique than in idea. What, one critic asks, is the tragedy ? Is it in the confusion of inner motive ? If so, it begins in the fifth act, and all else is epic preparation. Is it in the antagonism of sex, or is it in the clash of religions ? There is no unity of problem [1]. The same critic contends that the figure of Holofernes is neither dramatic nor tragic, but essentially lyric [2].

The first point may perhaps be met by the argument, implicit in what has been already said, that the opposition of two characters, each subject to the fate which makes their greatness antagonistic to each other and destructive to themselves, is, in itself, the tragedy. Confusion of motive, clash of sex, symbolic opposition of two religions—all these are included in the conflict of Judith and Holofernes. It is in this that Hebbel transforms the old story most radically. For the older poets and dramatists, Judith is a woman sure of victory, untouched by doubt, confident in her interpretation of God's will, like all the great men of her race. To Hebbel she is primarily a woman of complex nature, penalised by her own qualities, shaken and uprooted by the violence of the force which in her individual assertion she sets free.

The criticism of Holofernes, on the other hand, is supported by evidence of a decisive kind—the evidence of parody. Most, if not all, of the effectiveness of Nestroy's travesty depends on his caricature of Hebbel's tyrant ; but it is the element of exaggeration in the drawing of his character, rather than the lyrical or subjective conception of it, which lays it open to the parodist. ' Ich bin der

---

1. H. Meyer-Benfey : *Hebbels Dramen* Heft I (Judith) Göttingen, 1913, pp. 151-2 and passim.

2. H. Meyer-Benfey : *op. cit.*, p. 114.

Glanzpunkt der Natur. Noch hab ' ich keine Schlacht verloren,
ich bin die Jungfrau unter den Feldherrn. Ich möcht' mich einmal
mit mir selbst zusammenhetzen, nur um zu sehen, wer der stärkere
is, ich oder ich ' [1]. And when Idun says : ' Ich dachte nur— ',
Nestroy makes Holofernes exclaim : ' Das ist dein Verbrechen ;
ich allein denk ', und wer sich Gedanken anmasst, der begeht einen
Einbruch in meinen Kopf '. (sc. 21). A comparison with the
soliloquy of Holofernes and his speech to Judith (quoted above
pp. 98 & 99) shews this to be at once true parody and clever
criticism. The over-intensity of Holofernes is perhaps the chief
mark of immaturity in Hebbel's play ; and consequently the
burlesque of it is the most vital element of the Viennese parody,
which elsewhere (as in the story of the supposed Judith's marriage
with Manasses—sc. 24— or in the end, when the head of a sleeping
warrior is cut off, but he is discovered not to be Holofernes) is more
in the nature of farce.

Of much less interest than Nestroy's parody—which at least shews
that Hebbel's drama had life and interest for his age—is the translation of that same drama into iambic verse undertaken by Julius
Grosse in 1869. The passion of the Munich school of writers for
smooth verse and soothing rhetoric seems to have atrophied the
critical faculty of at least one of their number. Grosse, in his
Lebenserinnerungen notes as tasks of the year after he became
' Dramaturg ' of the Munich Hoftheater : ' ...die Wiederbelebung
und Bearbeitung älterer Werke...... endlich vor allen an erster
Stelle Hebbels *Judith.* '
' Die Bearbeitung von Raimunds grossem Zauberstück, sowie
die Umformung der modernen Prosa Hebbels in stilvollere
Diktion war die nächste Aufgabe des Sommers' [2]. In a Munich
' Theaterbericht ' of October 18th, 1868 (probably by Grosse)
a further explanation is given : ' Hebbels Prosa ist als
markig, eckig und " Shakespearisch " berühmt. Gleichwohl ist
sie in der Judith weder realistisch genug, um durch die Lokalfarbe
zu interessiren, wie z. B. im Goetheschen Götz, noch ideal genug,
um den durch und durch idealen Bau des Stücks genügend zu
bekleiden. Mit *einem* Wort, es fehlt der Sprache an jenem Adel

---

1. J. Nestroy : *Judith und Holofernes* sc. 3. in *Gesammelte Werke* herausgegeben
V. Chiavacci und L. Ganghofer. Lieferung 36. Stuttgart 1891. pp. 241-259.
2. *Ursachen und Wirkungen*, Braunschweig, 1896, p. 418.

und Kunststyl, welchen eine grosse Tragödie nicht entbehren kann ' [1]. The actors, however, refused to adopt the new version (already accepted by the Directors of the theatre)—not from artistic scruples, but for the reason that acceptance would have entailed the learning of new parts, which yet sufficiently resembled the old ones to make the task one of great difficulty [2]. The version was therefore laid aside, and appeared in 1870, with a dedication to Clara Ziegler emphasising once more the adapter's conviction of the suitability of verse for the drama. Grosse added to his initial crime by using the prompt-book (i. e. the theatre version, to which Hebbel expressly denied authority) as the basis for his adaptation; and, as might be expected, he did his best to convert the play into a series of solos and duets—thus providing a real ' Spielrolle ' or star-rôle for Judith [3]. Much in the great crowd scenes was cut as being too realistic ; and the end is in the spirit of the theatre version of Hebbel's play : Judith demands to be killed as a murderess (according to Jewish law) because she has been unmindful of her divine mission. The style, however, is the main thing for Grosse, as can be seen from his comments already quoted ; and the very fact of the conversion of Hebbel's prose into often mechanical iambic verse is enough to characterise the attempt.

During the latter half of the 19th century three narrative poems deal with the Judith story. Two of these—*Judith, or an old Picture of Absolutism re-touched*, an anonymous poem published in 1854, and *Judith*, the Seatonian prize poem of 1856, by the Rev. John Mason Neale, are written in a popular style resembling that of Scott's poetry. The first poem is undistinguished. It is in lines of four accents rhyming irregularly (often in couplets), and shews a curious lack of proportion in the treatment. The narrative follows the biblical original closely, but the length of the opening descriptions and preliminary speeches is comparatively great, while the episode of Achior's release is disposed of in two lines. Much is talked of, but little shewn in action. The writer is careful to

---

1. Quoted in the prefatory note to Grosse's *Judith* (Grosse : *Dramatische Werke*. Leipzig 1870, vol. VII, p. x) and in R. M. Werner : *Julius Grosses Judith*. Prager Deutsche Studien, vol. IX, II. Teil. Prag, 1908, p. 203.

2. v. *Ursachen und Wirkungen*, ed. cit. pp. 422-423.

3. v. *ibid*., and also R. M. Werner : *op. cit*. for a detailed analysis of Grosse's version.

proclaim Judith's feminine qualities ; as she is about to smite Holofernes, her tears, he says, are

> ' To woman's nature, not to mercy, due...
> Brief is the pause—ends now the awful strife,
> Truth's vindication calls—*her people's life* ' [1].

She is

> ' Merari's daughter—young Menasi's bride—
> Her wedded lord now parted from her side,
> From bridal gladness hurried to the tomb,
> Sun-stricken in the field at bright noon-tide—'   (p. 13).

Beyond this, the writer makes no contribution to the general
conception of Judith's character.

For some reason—perhaps this recent version—perhaps the
paucity of sacred subjects suitable for poetic treatment—Judith
was the subject set for the Seatonian Prize (carrying with it £40)
in 1856.   The Master of Arts who wrote the successful poem was
the Rev. John Mason Neale, of Trinity College, Cambridge ;
that he did not take the matter too seriously is evident from a
letter written on Nov. 8, 1856 to Benjamin Webb, a former fellow-
student and a life-long friend : ' It was a great joke, my getting
the Seatonian.   I began it on the Tuesday morning, and the fair
copy was finished on Wednesday evening.   So I bagged £38 net.
by two days' work '.   (' This ', says the editor of his *Letters*,
' was *Judith*, the fourth of his ten successful Seatonian poems ' [2]).
The treatment, as we should expect, is slight ; the poem consists
of eighteen short cantos in varying metres, and most of the narrative
is implied rather than actually related.   Cantos I to VIII are occupied with an opening apostrophe, a description of the conditions, an
account of the Edict of Nebuchadnezzar and an invocation to the
God of Israel.   Cantos IX and X give a picture of Bethulia under
siege, of the thirst which afflicts the people and of the tumult
prevailing in the city.   Canto XI tells how Ozias persuades the
people to wait for five days more.   Canto XII is devoted to Judith,
and Cantos XIII and XIV contain her speech to the citizens and
her prayer to God.   Canto XV introduces us to Holofernes, and we

---

1. *Judith*... London, 1854, p. 33.

2. *Letters of John Mason Neale*, D. D. Edited by his daughter (Mary Sackville
Lawson).   London, 1910, p. 279.

are witnesses of Judith's meeting with him. In the next canto the
passing of the five days is described, and in Canto XVII Holofernes
is dead and Judith has returned. The poem ends with a confession
of faith in the power of the Lord. The poet surmounts the difficulty
of the crisis by retrospective reflection :

> ' Great Holofernes is stretched in the dust ;
> He at a woman's feet bowed him and fell ;
> Him his own falchion has hurried to hell :
> He that o'er kindreds and nations had sway,
> He, whom the wide world had learned to obey,
> Found in the beauty of woman his lure—
> Found it and perished—and yet she is pure.'   (XVII)

This is an evasion ; and it is lyrical, as are all the more effective
moments of the poem. Judith herself is lyrically pourtrayed, in a
passage which is perhaps the one of greatest interest :

> ' Forth, as they spake such words of shame,
> In all her beauty, Judith came.
> Heav'n gave the far-off star its beam ;
> Earth's vapours feel and own its gleam :
> Heav'n sent amidst the angry press
> A vision of such loveliness—...
> ...And thus she stood amidst the strife,
> As one that came with words of life
> From God's celestial court.'   (XII)

There is a certain rapidity of movement which suits the cursory
treatment of the subject ; the writer has caught Scott's trick of
weaving in martial names and effective phrases :

> ' They come, convened by spell and ban,
> The nomad tribes of Turkistan :
> And Lydia's women-hearts are there,
> And Phrygia's sons their falchions bare.'   (V).

or again :

> ' On ancient gate, and terraced height,
> And bulwarks towering in their might.'   (I).

The poem is of Judith, not of Judith and Holofernes, and there is
little conception of a dramatic situation. It is definitely a lyrical
treatment, without trace of problem or conflict.

Very different in this respect is the latest of the narrative versions,

published in 1896—the *Judith and Holofernes* of Thomas Bailey
Aldrich.   Here the feeling for dramatic situation and the psychological interest are strongly marked, and it was doubtless this appreciation of the drama inherent in the subject which made the poet
consent to dramatise the poem in 1904.   Aldrich's chief interest
at first, however, was in his heroine.   In the Preface to the narrative
poem of 1896 he discusses her character, referring to the Greek and
Syriac versions of the story which differ from that of the Apocrypha.
Since the subject is ' fable and not history ', he allows himself some
dramatic liberties.   The Judith of the Apocrypha does not appeal
to him : ' she moves... a beautiful and cold-blooded abstraction,
with scarcely any feminine attribute except her religious fervour '.
In this point his criticism resembles that of Hebbel ; but he goes
on to point out the difference between Judith and Charlotte Corday [1],
despite their identity of motive, and concludes: ' Judith's character
throughout the ancient legend lacks that note of tenderness with
which the writer has here attempted to accent her heroism ' [2].
This attempt is marked at once, for Aldrich adds a new motive to
the story :

> ' That night she held long vigil in the tower,
> Merari's daughter, dead Manasseh's wife,
> Who, since the barley harvest when he died,
> Had dwelt three years a widow in her house,
> And looked on no man : where Manasseh slept,
> In his strait sepulchre, there slept her heart.
> Yet dear to her, and for his memory dear
> Was Israel...'   (Book I).

It is love for Manasseh which inspires her faith and prompts her
to service.   Her main attribute is faith, immediately emphasised
in the subsequent lines :

> ' ...Hither had she come
> To pray in the still starlight, far from those
> Who watched or wept in the sad world below ;
> And in the midnight, in the tower alone,
> She knelt and prayed as one that doubted not : '

Following on her prayer is a description of the trance into which
she falls ; and it is in treating this mystical aspect of her character

---

1. It seems probable that Aldrich is here definitely referring to Hebbel's judgment
on Judith. v. supra, p. 96.
2. T. B. Aldrich : *Judith and Holofernes*. Boston and New York, 1896. p. VI.

that Aldrich shews the keenest insight and the greatest sympathy.
The atmosphere of her mysterious vision is suggested :

> ' And while she wept, bowed like a lotus flower
> That leans to its own shadow in the Nile,
> A strangest silence fell upon the land ;
> Like to a sea-mist spreading east and west
> It spread....................... then the world
> Crumbled and vanished, and nought else she knew. '   (Book I).

' Now after that she had ceased to cry unto the God of Israel,
and had made an end of all these words, She rose where she had
fallen down... ', runs the original (X, 1-2) ; this is interpreted as
the bewildered return of the spirit to the body :

> ' And Judith stood bewildered, with flusht cheek
> Prest to the stonework.   When she knelt to pray
> It was dead night, and now ' twas break of dawn ;
> Yet had not sleep upon her eyelids set
> Its purple seal...
> So all her thought lay tangled in her brain,
> And what had chanced eluded memory. '   (Book I).

The wonder and beauty of her face issue from this inner light of
faith ; the Elders of the city marvel as she passes that there is

> ' ...one face left not hunger-pinched, or wan
> With grief's acquaintance...
> And white-haired Charmis looked on her and said :
> " This woman walketh in the light of God ". '

Judith's reply characterises her still further :

> ' " Would it were so ! " said Judith.   " I know not ;
> But this I know, that where faith is, is light.
> Let us not doubt Him !   If we doubt we die ". '

Thus, strong in faith, she sets her face towards the camp of
Holofernes.

It is interesting to note how the poet, with this predominantly
mystical conception of Judith's character, presents her in her
intercourse with Holofernes. For his Judith can be neither
triumphant victor nor beguiling beauty ; his problem is to reconcile
the tenderness of the first book with the necessary horror of the
third. Aldrich links them by the second book, ' The Camp of

Asshur ', which presents the dramatic situation.   Holofernes and
his captains are engaged in hot debate ; tempers are fierce and
quarrels imminent.   The effect of Judith's appearance is instant-
aneous and miraculous :

> ' ...   ...suddenly each blade
> Slipt back to sheath, and the pale captains stood |
> Transfixt'...

One glimpse of her—who is ' appalled at sight of all those angry
lords '—

> ' And Holofernes ' voice took softer tone '.

Judith's tale—the story of sin and profanation in Bethulia, and
the prophecy of victory for Holofernes— ' is told, while Holofernes
gazes on her beauty ' filled with passion and with love.   Only at
one point, when Holofernes promises that if her prophecy is fulfilled
she shall live in splendour with him at Nineveh, do her sex and race
conquer her for a moment :

> ' Then on her cheek the ripe blood of her race
> Faltered an instant ;

but   ' Even as thou wilt
> So would thy servant',   she replies.

Her personality obsesses Holofernes.   He who in the opening
was pictured as crossing the Euphrates

> ' Unheralded, like some tornado, loosed
> Out of the brooding hills... '

and striding through the tents cursing

> ' ...the doting gods, who gave no aid,
> But slumbered somewhere in their house of cloud '   (Book I)

is now seen to hold himself aloof, speaking little with his chiefs,
sleeping fitfully that night,

> ' ...tormented by a dream
> That ever waked him'.

In the third book the crisis of the conflict is related.   It opens
with a vivid description of Holofernes, terror-struck at a dream :

> ' The hates and cruel passions of his youth

> Became incorporate and immortal things,
> With tongue to blazon his eternal guilt '.

It is the influence of Judith's purity whence this terror is born; a dim oppressive feeling lies heavy upon him :

> ' Is it an omen that the end draws nigh ?
> Such things foretell the doom of fateful men '.

But when he realises that Bagoas sees him as he starts up in terror, anger rises in him :

> ' Then Holofernes could have struck the slave
> Dead in his path—what man had ever seen
> The Prince of Asshur tremble ?

Pride and defiance are fundamental in him ; he bids Judith to the banquet, in spite of dreams and omens :

> ' ...What matters, when the strong gods call,
> Whether they find a man at feast or prayer ? '

And he finds the woman's submissive answer to his invitation well :

> ' "Were this not so "' he mused,, " would not my name '
> Be as a jest and gibe, mong womenkind ?
> Maidens would laugh behind their unbound hair ".

The character of Holofernes is thus set for the tragedy ; the picture of him in the Camp, proud, despotic, of ungovernable mind, is now supplemented by this view of him at grips with passion and foreboding. At this point the poet turns again to Judith, who accepts the invitation with a smile, but prays :

> ' O save me, Lord, from this dark cruel prince,
> And from mine own self save me ; for this man,
> A worshipper of fire and senseless stone,
> Slayer of babes upon the mother's breast,
> He, even he, hath by some conjurer's trick,
> Or by his heathen beauty, in me stirred
> Such pity as stays anger's lifted hand.
> O let not my hand falter, in Thy name !
> ...Since Thou hast sent the burden, send the strength ! '

---

1. This is an expansion of the original (v. Book of Judith, ch. XII, 12).

This prayer of Judith's is crucial, for it reveals the conflict in her, as Aldrich conceives it—a conflict between pity (and something of a softer feeling) for Holofernes, and the pity inspired by Bethulia (partly dependent, as was seen in the first book, on her love for the dead Manasseh, together with her steadfast faith). The poet concentrates on the pourtrayal of this conflict in Judith's spirit, for it is by means of it that he presents his characteristic view of her. While waiting to be led in to Holofernes, she comforts Marah, her servant, smiling and whispering ' It is well ' ; but later

> ' ...paling, whispered ' Fail me not !... '

The analysis of her state of mind when she has lulled the prince to sleep with wine and song amplifies the picture :

> ' And Judith looked on him, and pity crept
> Into her bosom.   The ignoble sleep
> Robbed not his pallid brow of majesty
> Nor from the curved lip took away the scorn ;
> These rested still...
> O broken sword of proof !   O prince betrayed !
> Her he had trusted, he who trusted none.
> The sharp thought pierced her, and her breast was torn,
> And half she longed to bid her purpose die,
> To stay, to weep, to kneel down at his side
> And let her long hair trail upon his face.
> Then Judith dared not look upon him more,
> Lest she should lose her reason through her eyes ; '

With a natural gesture she covers up her eyes to shut him out. But she cannot shut him out from ' that subtler sight within ', and so she stands, irresolute.   The suddenly she hears the moan of children and women in despair, and

> ' ...all the woes
> Of the doomed city pleaded at her heart'.

Hurriedly, on impulse, she blows out all the lights save one, takes the faulchion from its nail and smites him thrice and flings the blade away.   Then she and Marah flee in fear,

> ' Wild with the pregnant horrors of the night '

and hurl themselves against the city gates.

Meanwhile the poet pictures the dead quiet of the Assyrian camp, broken by the story of an Arab scout of a head set on the city gate—

a head he vaguely knows. Bagoas, troubled, seeks to wake Holofernes ; when no answer comes

> '   ...Bagoas stoopt
> And softly lifting up the damask cloth
> Beheld the prince of Asshur lying dead '.

Terrible his cry rings out, like that of a leopard pinioned by a
falling tree ' in some breathless wilderness at night '—panic and
battle ensue, Bethulia is saved

> ' ...through God's grace, that nerved a gentle hand,
> Not shaped to wield the deadly blade of war '.

Love and honour wait on Judith's steps ; the years come lightly
to her.

> ' Many desired her, but she put them by
> With sweet denial : where Manasseh slept
> In his strait sepulchre, there slept her heart.
> And there beside him, in the barley-field,
> Nigh unto Dothaim, they buried her. '

The emphasis throughout is thus on the idea that Judith loses
no womanly quality by being the pure channel of the will of God—a
complete contrast to the conception of Hebbel, who finds it impossible to reconcile her mission and her sex. Both poets agree in
rejecting the Apocryphal figure ; but Aldrich refuses to picture
Judith as incurring tragic guilt by her action. It is of great interest
therefore to examine his dramatisation of *Judith and Holofernes*,
undertaken at the request of Miss Nance O'Neil and published
in 1904 as *Judith of Bethulia*. The title suggests a concentration
of interest in Judith herself which is (when compared with the title
of Aldrich's narrative poem) a curious reversal of the usual practice
in epic and dramatic poetry respectively. The poet entitles the
play ' A Tragedy '—a title which further illustrates his view of
Judith's character, but which is not perhaps entirely convincing.
It is interesting, however, to find certain slight changes in the
figure of the heroine which emphasise the pathos (if not the tragedy)
of her situation. Whereas in the poem she is pictured as living,
serene though sorrowful, honoured and beloved, until she is buried
by Manasseh's side, in the drama she appears in the last scene,
broken down and pale, in widows' weeds, refusing the homage

proffered her, until she is persuaded to accept it for the sake of
others :

> ' From this day forth I dwell apart, alone
> In mine own house where laughter may not come
> Nor any light, vain voices of the world.
> Only the sorrowful shall find the door
> Unbarred and open.
>   In thy memory
> Keep me as some belovèd wife or child,
> Or sister that died long and long ago !'   (IV, I).

And as Achior (whose love for her is an important element in the
dramatic situation) attempts to follow her, she hastily says :

> ' Let no one born of woman follow me ! '

Here a more intense conflict seems to be indicated than in the
poem ; or at least its effect on Judith is more suggestive of intensity.
Her action in slaying Holofernes is utterly at variance with the
instincts of her nature ; hence she feels that life in her is extinct,
and sorrow her portion.   Nathan voices her problem :

> ' To think a woman did it !   Day of days !
> Yet is not Judith made of tenderness ?
> ......
> I wonder, now, the peril being past
> And all her pulses stilled, if in her thought
> There is not some vague, nameless sense of dread
> Of her own self that could do such a deed ! '   (IV, I)

But Joachim, another scholar of Bethulia, answers with the
amazement of the simple when confronted with the subtler mind :

> ' O Nathan, son of Paul, thou ever wert
> A splitter of fine hairs !   Had she not slain
> That monster in his hour of victory,
> Making his pride to bite the very dust,
> What had become of *thee*, and all of us ! '   (IV, I)

The presentation of the two points of view—that of Judith and
that of the average Bethulian—by two minor characters is an
effective dramatic touch.   Her conflict with herself at the moment
of achievement is emphasised in the stage directions as well as in
her monologue (which corresponds in the main to that in the
narrative poem) ; she is shewn rushing wildly into the tent, and

violently thrusting aside the draperies as she emerges (III, 2).   She invokes the memory of Jael to nerve her hand to action, and triumphantly exclaims that the Lord has heard her prayer.

Apart from the amplification of the picture of Judith, the main additions made by Aldrich in the dramatic version are in the rôles of Achior and Bagoas.   The former is described in the list of dramatis personae as ' The Ammonite, lately fled from Holofernes and in love with Judith' ; the whole episode of Achior's tale to Holofernes and his consequent exile is omitted, and he first appears, waiting for Judith when she descends from her night's vigil in the tower.   His love for her is plainly indicated ; his argument with her enhances the dramatic effect of the mysterious vision she relates, and of her resolve to pursue her hidden plan.   ' In other days ', he tells her,

> ' I served Prince Holofernes, from whose wrath I fled
> To dwell, a wanderer, in alien tents,
> And since have set my breast against his spears '.   (I, 2)

and Judith, in her speech with Holofernes in Act II, makes use of Achior's previous prophecy to the Assyrian captain.   Forbidden to go with her on an errand he knows to be fraught with danger, Achior resolves to follow her into the hostile camp in the hope of rescuing her [1].   Judith, by disowning him and feigning indifference, allays the suspicions of Holofernes, and Achior is led off by the guard, only to reappear at the end in Bethulia after being set free by Bagoas.   His love is then finally rejected by Judith in her resolve to live apart.

Bagoas, ' Captive and slave to Holofernes ', plays an unusual rôle in Aldrich's drama.   He it is who enables Judith to mix a sleeping potion with Holofernes' wine ; he falls in love with her, and endeavours thus to save her from the ' pitiless love ' of Holofernes.   A short indication of his former station is given in his first conversation with Judith (II, 2), and this explains his attitude to Holofernes, which is one of fear and distrust.   By his agency (and at Judith's request) Achior is set free when panic seizes the Assyrians, and is thus enabled to lead the charge against the latter. In these two characters Aldrich has deviated most markedly from his source, and it is presumably to them that he refers in a prefatory

---

1. In this one incident, Achior plays a part similar to that of Ephraim in Hebbel's drama—but without a similar effect on Judith's mind.   Achior appears as a lover of Judith in several modern versions, v. infra, pp. 121, 133-134.

note where he declares the drama to be a distinct work ' dealing with characters, incidents, and situations not to be found in the poem or in the apocryphal episode upon which both pieces were based '.

The populace of Bethulia plays a more important part in the drama than in the poem ; the first scene of the second act depicts the misery and thirst which afflict the citizens, and the general appeal is concentrated for Judith in the figure of her old nurse Naomi, whose reason has fled under the stress of sorrow.   Aldrich's picture of the suffering multitude is idealised—their sensibilities have not been blunted by physical miseries, and the scene has pathos rather than tragic verisimilitude [1].   It is in striking contrast to the great scene in Hebbel's *Judith* ; there are shewn the rebellion and turbulence of the distracted crowd, their changeable resolves, quick anger and resentment, their credulity and passions—a picture of the nakedness of human souls in misery and despair.   Aldrich sees the idyllic side in the crowd, as he sees it in the figure of Judith in the narrative poem.

On the whole therefore—apart from the omissions and concentrated exposition necessarily demanded by the dramatic form— *Judith of Bethulia* shews mainly a certain expansion of Judith's character, a dramatisation of her conflict, and the addition of two considerable episodes contributing to the main action of the play. It is interesting chiefly because it succeeds to a certain extent in a sympathetic presentation of Judith as a religious messenger, and in imparting interest to this presentation.   Whereas in the early dramas this interest is less strong, and in modern dramatic treatments Judith incurs tragic guilt in the course of her action (or, in 20th century versions, merely acts in obedience to suppressed or unacknowledged instinct), Aldrich makes a bold endeavour to retain the purity of her motives and character while making her a more subtle and interesting dramatic figure than the mere ' instrument ' of earlier religious drama.   He is not entirely successful in creating a tragedy (as the title would suggest the play to be) ; for the conflict of Judith's nature and her message seems just to fall short of real tragic force.   But there is without doubt sufficient dramatic interest in the pourtrayal of her character to make her attractive, if not arresting.

---

1. It may be noted that even in the minor versions published since 1914, the populace is pourtrayed more realistically.

That the modern interest of the story centres in the psychological conflict in Judith at the moment of her action is once more demonstrated by the one-act play of Mr. T. Sturge Moore, published in 1911 and performed by the Stage Society in January, 1916.   Here is an attempt to dramatise, not a story but an impression—Judith in the performance of her deed.   Consequently the poet's art is concentrated entirely on two things—on conveying the atmosphere of a brooding Eastern night, a setting for the sharp crisis of action that cuts across its voluptuous ease, and on pourtraying the state of mind in Judith which leads up to that crisis. Bagoas, the weird figure of a fat old eunuch, Adonikam the boy, precocious with the early ripeness of the south, the black slaves who act as torch-bearers, all help to create the atmosphere of sensuous charm. Three dialogues, a monologue, and a final conversation between Bagoas and Judith (with her handmaid Mira) make up the dramatic sketch.   The first dialogue, between Bagoas and the boy, serves to set the key, and the child's report of the dancing of the ' Hebrew sorceress' is a miniature of the main picture of Judith's intercourse with Holofernes which immediately succeeds it.   Gradually the Assyrian becomes intoxicated by the charms of sense, until he becomes actually so by tasting Judith's wine. She chants and croons and bewitches him, until by a mere look she banishes a momentary dread which comes upon him at the thought of being alone, intoxicated, at her mercy :

> ' Forgive a queer chill thought that from the moon
> Entered the tent despite of thy sweet singing. '   (p. lix)

She answers him :

> ' A lover's thoughts should be red as dark wine '

then, crooning and stepping rhythmically,

> ' Drink, drink, and drink again.
> There is no other end of pain. '

Holofernes gradually falls asleep ; and Judith appears at the tent door, looks up at the stars and in a long rhythmic monologue works herself up to action. This is the point of psychological interest in the play. She is uncertain ; or rather she is, although

convinced of her mission, unable at first to put compulsion on
herself :

> ' Now is the time to help me ;
> Thou hast seen me, O Lord God ;
> He did not touch me to defile me, and he sleeps :
> Thou puttedst this deed in my heart to do,
> ...Alas, I am alone,
> Alone, in this huge night.
> Ah, what am I to do ? '   (p. lx)

The poetic nature in her adds to the complexity of her problem :

> ' The most that can be done, the best, is like
> A single point of light, a lonely star ; '

Darkness wraps her spirit round :

> '   ...O God, it is thy will,
> That didst create the evil and the good.
> Pour thou thy strength into my weakness now ;
> Pierce thou my life's obscurity at once '.   (p. lxi)

She interrupts herself to fetch the faulchion from the tent, and
it now acts as accompaniment to the remainder of her monologue ;
her imagination pictures the details of the deed in all their horror,
her heart rebels at the cruelty which is so repugnant to her nature —
who had been ' praised for loving tenderness '. But finally she
prays :

> ' Be present with me now !
> For the exaltation of thy people aid me now,
> Approver of the righteous will that livest
> Even in a woman's heart '.   (p. lxii)

She re-enters the tent, where a groan from Holofernes and a cry
from Judith indicate the action, while outside two drunken captains
enter and vow vengeance on Holofernes for enjoying the delights
he has forbidden to the army.   From this point to the end, where
Bagoas speeds Judith and Mira on their way and envies Holofernes
his sound sleep—' What ease health hath, contentment how it
sleeps ! ' (p. lxxii)—the dramatic irony is sharp. When the
danger of detection by the captains is over, the silence is broken
by ' the sound of an agony of weeping from within the tent ',
which ' as briefly subsides '. Mira in terror comes to call her
mistress, and Judith appears with altered voice and countenance.

She feels—as did Hebbel in conceiving his Judith—that only a
peculiar situation, a special preparation, could fit any woman for
the task she has fulfilled :

> ' O, thou didst widow me unto this end !
> No maid had known all this, and no wife could
> Have left her husband for a work like mine.
> > ...O God,
> My weak estate proved strength—that I grieved for,
> With that thou didst begird Manasses' widow ;
> She grieved to think her husband such a man
> As this bland easy-going Holofernes ;
> She grieved to lose so kind and fond a husband :
> Yea, both these griefs did long time suck my heart,
> My childless heart, my widowed childless heart.
> They were thy preparation for this deed ; '

She vows to live henceforth dedicated to God, to pine no more for
children, since the memory of her deed shall live with her, shall be
her daughter, shall

> '   ...become a nobler woman
> Than she who thought God had allotted her
> A life already spoiled... '   (pp. lxvi-lxvii)

There is here a wealth of suggestion as to Judith's character and
history. We see her as one disappointed by life—not, as with
Hebbel, by an enigma, but by a human failing in her husband as
well as by her childlessness—given to introspection and reflection,
yet called upon to do a deed where both these tendencies increase
the horror tenfold. The contrast between the atmosphere of
Holofernes' camp—its heat and lust—with Judith's vow to bathe
at dawn in the cool river, skilfully suggests an innate antagonism
between the Assyrian and the daughter of Israel ; and it is significant that this Judith is not touched by love for Holofernes—though
the latter is by no means drawn as a repellent character. Her
conflict is purely one of natural feeling and the conviction of her
mission, of sensitive imagination and the crude horror of actual
necessity.

It is, plainly, a picture above all that the poet gives us in this
one-act play. One reviewer calls it ' a plastic and splendid picture
to which the words formed an accompaniment ' [1]. Dramatically,

---

1. *Sunday Times.* — 30 Jan. 1916.

this description, with its implied censure of the lack of action, is no doubt correct. From the point of view of a treatment of Judith's character, of the relation in her of action to character, it does the play perhaps rather less than justice.

The latest dramatic version of the story in England dates from 1919, when Mr. Arnold Bennett published *Judith*. A Play in Three Acts, Founded on the apocryphal book of ' Judith '. This play was performed at Eastbourne in April of that year and published at the end of the month. The title indicates that there is nothing revolutionary in the treatment of the story. But although the author keeps closely to the outlines of the original narrative, he makes some changes in the characters, and more especially in the minor ones. Ozias in particular is elaborated and altered from the colourless figure of the original. The first act, which takes place in a street of Bethulia outside Judith's house, is virtually a duologue between Ozias and Judith, for it is entirely occupied with their relationship. Incidentally, almost, the various elements in the general situation are shewn, and the maddening thirst of the populace, their consequent greed, selfishness and deceit, form a dark background to the action. The old man Chabris, with his ' pitiless memory ' and complete self-centredness, outdoes Ozias in his greed for water ; the soldier lies, denying that the guard has anything to drink, for Ozias ' in seemliness asks for a lie, and that which he asks is given to him—in seemliness ' (1,.1). Ozias loves Judith, and all his being is centred in the desire for her and for aggrandisement. Proud, vainglorious, deceitful, he yet has impulses of a better sort when dominated by her presence : thus he looses Achior's bonds at her request, though jealous that the request is made, and her stronger will, her beauty and persuasiveness induce him to allow her to go forth from the city on her secret errand. Meanwhile, the figure of Achior, episodic though it be, has gained a certain importance. Judith has vouched for his truthfulness and honour ; Ozias has released him from bondage at her request, and obvious complications may ensue. At the end of the act Judith passes through the opened gates ; they are closed again behind her and the watch-fires lit.

The second act is occupied entirely with the relations between Judith and Holofernes, and the whole crisis of the action is contained in it. Haggith—the Abra of the original—has more to do than in the majority of versions. She prepares the way for Judith and advertises her advent ; and her beguilement of Ingur is a foil to the more subtle beguilement of Holofernes by her mistress. Though talkative and indiscreet, she plays her part well, and finds the befooling of a man simpler than she had pictured it to be.

The character of Bagoas is fully developed and altered in this act, as was that of Ozias in Act I. Instead of the mere attendant of the earlier versions, the cynical slave of later ones, or the accomplice (as in Aldrich's play), the dramatist here presents the complete sycophant—vain, ambitious, servile and tyrannical. He and his subordinates demonstrate the corruption and tyranny of Holofernes ' camp ; his immediate antagonism to Judith proceeds from his perception of the power which her beauty will exercise over Holofernes and the prejudicial effect that this will have on his own position, as well as on their plans. Judith tries to propitiate him ; but her most effective weapon is her immediate success in enslaving Holofernes. The prince is inflammable, spoilt by power and Eastern corruption, wilful as a child and despotic to all but Judith, to whom he can deny nothing ; but he is at no time a repellent character. At moments he is even attractive in his intercourse with Judith ; in the final scene of the second act, where she first beguiles and then kills him, his passion for her endows him with an almost child-like tenderness.

Judith herself is a complex personality. Irony is the keynote of the author's pourtrayal of her ; it is best expressed in her murmured speech as she slays and caresses Holofernes—a speech which at one and the same time expresses her resentment at being compelled to use guile and deceit and makes us wonder whether this resentment is genuine. There is something repellent in Judith's efficiency in combining caressing flattery with murderous intent. Just so does she rebuke Ozias with authority in the first act, and in the last act resolve to wed Achior in spite of the former's opposition. This Judith is no prey to nerves or to compunction ; decisive, compelling, supremely competent in attaining her desires, she does not stir our sympathies ; indeed, in the last scene, the braggart, deceitful Ozias commands them in his defeat rather than Judith in her triumphant assertion of her right to wed Achior. Her last remark savours not a little of the irony which characterises her throughout : Ozias leaves Bethulia for Jerusalem with a final boast as to his delivery of Israel, and Judith replies : ' The lord Ozias is called to greatness. Peace go with him '.

The time element in this version is worthy of note. A day and a half elapse between Acts I and II—that is, between Judith's departure from Bethulia and her arrival in Holofernes' camp. A night and a morning intervene between her departure from the camp and her triumphant entry into Bethulia (heralded, some hours previously, by Haggith). Thus the traditional period of five days is almost occupied, but Judith only spends one day in the Assyrian camp, and leaves it that same night—a proceeding which makes her beguiling of Holofernes no less credible and considerably facilitates the keeping of her law, but which does not tend to make her more easily intelligible to us.

Since adaptability is plainly characteristic of the Judith theme throughout its history, it is not surprising to find modern versions of it based on Freudian theory. Georg Kaiser, in *Die jüdische Witwe*, has made of it a ' Fleischkomödie ' (in the language of a modern historian of drama [1]) whose most salient characteristic is its treatment of the sexual problem. This problem is indicated in Hebbel's play (and in this respect, as has been noted, his treatment is singular and characteristic), but whereas there the motive is related to the whole personality of Judith, is shewn in its reaction upon her nature and traditions, here no such complexity is admitted. The play revolves around Judith's desire ; and this provides the only motivisation it can boast. The primary force of her character dominates the action ; history is a matter of obedience to it, and Holofernes, Nebukadnezar (and others) are but so many puppets dancing to her will. The dramatist is conscious of presenting the story in a new light, for the appropriate motto is prefixed : ' Oh, meine Brüder, zerbrecht, zerbrecht mir die alten Tafeln ! ' True to psycho-analytic principles, the dramatist seeks the motive of Judith's acts in the history of her youth. Act I shews us the child of twelve brought to the temple by mother and sister to celebrate her marriage with Manasse—the old, repellent scribe, who tries to preserve the appearance of youth by artificial means. The chief part of this act is devoted to the overcoming of Judith's inarticulate resistance, which is not lessened by the sight of her bridegroom, granted as a special concession to her youth and her unwillingness. The materialist preoccupations of the merchants, the servile adulation displayed towards the scribes, the absorption of the women in the obligation of marriage and child-bearing, the

---

1. K. Holl : *Geschichte des deutschen Lustspiels.* Leipzig, 1923, p. 337.

general impression of a festival of sex and commerce are vividly
conveyed in the dialogue.   Above all, the senile lust of Manasse
is emphasised ; and this links the first with the second act, which
is devoted to the elaboration of this theme, and to the pourtrayal
of its effect on Judith.   In the third act, the city is in a stage of
siege, and Judith has been left a widow by the death of Manasse ;
only five days' provisions remain before the town must surrender
to the enemy.   All through the siege only one impulse, one preoccupation is alive in Judith's mind : she, whom Manasse has
left barren, must receive her right.   Isaschar, the aged scribe who
comes to persuade her with cunning to give up to him the books of
Manasse, that he may find the prescription in them for the ' special
purification ' that will make him safe in the day of the wrath of the
Lord, sends to her Chabri and Charmi, younger elders of the city,
who yet fail her.   She hears that the enemy are strong because
they have no women in their camps, and their strength proceeds
from their desire [1].   She therefore determines to seek out the enemy,
and at the close of the act she leaves her house for the hostile camp.
Only in Act IV does the scene change from the city to the Assyrian
camp, where the decisive action takes place as an episode in Judith's
quest.   Disguised as a boy she has penetrated into the camp, and
is discovered in the opening scene by a captain, who reports the
fact to Holofernes.   The Assyrian situation is made clear by the
dialogue of Nebukadnezar, the young, effeminate king, chiefly
preoccupied with his dreams and their interpretation, Holofernes,
the strong, brutal general of the army, and Achior, by whose
advice Judith is allowed to live and is brought in to Holofernes.
Judith however is more attracted by Nebukadnezar than by Holofernes, and after sitting at an elaborate banquet with the general,
she cuts off his head in order to win Nebukadnezar.   The latter's
courage evaporates at such a deed, and he flees from the tent,
startling the whole army into panic flight, and bewildering Judith,
who remains, frustrated in her purpose.

The fifth act shews the citizens assembled in rejoicing at the
temple, where the head of Holofernes hangs, to celebrate the miracle
of its rescue and to hold a service of dedication and thanksgiving.
Judith, hailed as the saviour of her people, miraculously preserved

---

1. The contrast between the ' weiblose Krieger ' and the effeminate Jews is
similar to that in Kaiser's *Europa* (Berlin 1915). (v. Act V, where the contrast is
most clearly drawn).

from sin, is to be consecrated to celibacy and to the service of the Lord. The opening scene of the play is here repeated, with ironic intention—Judith is led in again, after a year has elapsed, by her kindred, her resistance is once more overcome, and she is conducted into the Holy of Holies by the High Priest of Jerusalem, as reward for her great deed. Thus beginning and end are contrasted ; the repetition of the situation with complete reversal of its meaning and its purpose points the comedy of this conception ; but at the end there are indications that the virile manhood of the priest fulfils Judith's desire.

The structure of the play is loose ; only the continuity of Judith's impulse through the changing situations gives it unity. This unity is comic, for always her impulse guides her action and, until the end, she is invariably disappointed in her expectations. The contrast between appearance and reality is thus used to make comedy out of a theme, hitherto usually considered to be epic, narrative, or tragic [1]. Similarly, the dramatist breaks new ground in his use of episodes, both new and traditional. The part of Achior, while it occupies less space and attention than in the majority of versions, is considerably altered. Achior only appears in person in the fourth act, when he gives a decisive turn to the action by representing to Holofernes the power which will be his over the Israelite city, if Judith can be made to sin against the racial exclusiveness ordained by Israel's God. Here he plays in part the traditional rôle of the Ammonite chieftain in warning Holofernes of the power of Jehovah ; but it is related in a new way to the appearance of Judith among the Assyrians, and he plays skilfully on the superstitious element in Holofernes' character—an element further exploited by Nebukadnezar, whose rôle is expanded beyond recognition. Achior's motives are not entirely disinterested, and Holofernes sends him (again partially in conformity with tradition) to proclaim to the Israelites their imminent defeat. After this, we only hear of Achior from one of the populace in the fifth act, where his doings are narrated as a commentary on the miracle of Judith's state. This concentration and re-moulding, in which the dramatist retains the traditional form, as it were, and supplies a new content, uses the main events of the episode but re-interprets them in different terms, illustrate what Kaiser has done with the

---

1. It is of interest to compare Kaiser's similar treatment of an equally well-known theme in *König Hahnrei*.

whole story and with every figure in it. That in so doing he follows a present-day tendency is evident ; further corroboration may be found (outside Germany and England) in a criticism lately published concerning the *Judith* of Henry Bernstein [1]. The critic here analyses the psychology of Judith, whose chief characteristic in the drama under discussion is violence ; he finds the motive force of this in woman's revolt against love—a post-war pheno-menon. Since in this she remains unenfranchised, still ' possessed ', she despises it for the humiliation it inflicts upon her new independ-ence ; and thus Judith's violence against Holofernes embodies a fundamental conflict of sex, pride replacing love in woman. An intellectual is substituted for a physical basis in this analysis ; but the fact remains the same : that the story of Judith is being continually re-interpreted in the light of the most modern theorising and the latest quasi-scientific generalisations [2].

An interesting modern version of the story, free from the prevail-ing preoccupation with Judith's unconscious self, is that of Otto Burchard : *Judith und Holofernes*, ein patriotisches Schauspiel in fünf Aufzügen. Written in blank verse of considerable beauty, this version shews a distinct sense of the dramatic and poetic value of the tale ; in spite of its sub-title and the date of its publication (1915) it displays no tendency to let propaganda outweigh dramatic proportion, or to sacrifice poetic to political aims.

The character of Achior in this version has far more intellectual interest and importance than usual ; and it is significant that the action opens and closes with scenes in which he plays a pro-minent part. He fulfils the traditional rôle in creating an impression of the might and ruthlessness of Holofernes, and he does this with great dramatic effect in the first and second scenes. The play opens with a scene in which he appears wounded, just exiled from the camp of Holofernes, and uncertain what reception awaits him in Bethulia. Two citizens support him with difficulty to the well, which is close to Judith's house, and after he has given an

1. Gaston Rageot in *Revue Bleue*, Nov. 4. 1922, pp. 707-708.

2. An interesting oontrast to Kaiser's view of the Judith story is to be found in Hans Kyser's *Titus und die Jüdin*, which also appeared in 1911. Here a woman's refusal to imitate the act of Judith is the central point in the drama. Titus, resolved on the destruction of Jerusalem, falls in love with a Jewess, and gives her the power to bring about peace. She chooses this, and resists the appeal to kill Titus, as Judith killed Holofernes ; therefore the Jews, on her return with an offering of bread to the starving city, stone her to death, because she has not followed the illustrious example of her predecessor.

account of the events leading up to his exile, they call in Judith's help to revive him.   An opportunity is thus given for Judith's appearance, and her first speech at once enlists our sympathy :

> Ich seh, dass er aus fremdem Lande stammt.
> Hätt' ihn der Herr geschickt, er wär willkommen.
> Doch da ein andrer Gott ihn so verliess,
> So lern er unsres Gottes Gnade kennen,
> Die er ihm schenkt, obgleich von ihm verschmäht.

At once there follows the first mention of Holofernes : Achior says :

> Da hilft kein Gott, wo Holofernes wütet.
> Auch nicht der Deine !—

and the sharp contrast of scepticism and belief is drawn — a contrast which it is partly the aim of the drama to resolve.   Judith takes Achior into her house to nurse him ; and in the third scene she questions him about Holofernes.   His replies convey adequately the terror of the tyrant, and she finally demands, in words which suggest her own essential humanity—already demonstrated in action— :

> Ist das ein Mensch, der solche Frevel zeugte ?

In the next scene, Gothoniel recognises Achior, and the latter relates his tale to the Bethulian elders ; by an effective dramatic device he expands his narrative in the face of Osias' unbelief. Judith is full of confidence that God will grant the victory to His people, and persuades the elders to defend the town.   At this moment one of her shepherds rushes in to tell her that her flocks have been seized by robbers : and Achior exclaims :

> Das war kein Räuber, Holofernes tat's.

From all sides news of fresh calamities pours in, and the impression of Holofernes is thus dramatically confirmed.   Prayers (in lyric measures) are offered up in Bethulia, and the first act closes on this note of trust and confidence in God.

Act II opens with a scene between two Bethulian soldiers, deserters, who plan to steal the consecrated wine.   Their reasons fro deserting give the exposition of the situation ; it is the fifth day of the siege, there is no water in the beleaguered city and the enemy has advanced almost to the gates.   Achior surprises them

and rebukes them ; but in a monologue in the succeeding s ene he
gives expression to his own despair.   Here again he is intellectually
interesting ; he reflects on the nature of belief, and rebels against
the forsaking of Judith by her God, in spite of her faith in Him.
Achior's description of Judith mirrors her state of mind with great
skill ; indeed he is the only person in the drama who is capable
of appreciating her to the full.   The third scene is important in the
development of the action.   Achior gives an account of the reverses
suffered by the Bethulians, of the embassy sent to Holofernes and
of his reply.   The women of the city are to be allowed to pass out
freely : the men must become slaves to him.   Abra breaks into
lamentation, and Achior attempts to console her ; Judith, who
has only spoken five times, and then only to ask short questions,
suddenly turns away and re-enters the house, and Abra is called
to her to act as tire-woman.   The act closes on the note of Achior's
doubt ; he thinks that after all Judith stands in little need of the
comfort he has been preparing to give her :

> War das die Keuschheit, die sie schwur,
> Als einst Manasse sterbend von ihr schied ?
> ....,.....
> Einst starb mir Ammon, der gehörnte König,
> Der unsres Volkes mächtge Gottheit war.
> Doch als ich Judith heut verstummen sah,
> Ward mir gewiss, dass auch Jehovah starb.   (II, 5)

Thus to Achior, faith in Judith and belief in God have become
indissolubly connected.

With the third act, the scene of action is transferred to the camp
of Holofernes, where the council of generals is just at an end.   The
dramatist at once indicates the character of Holofernes, who decides
that he will kill all the men of Bethulia on their surrender ' to save
them from slavery ', and that he will allow the women free egress
—so far.   There must, he says, be relaxation for his warriors ;
therefore only the old men, frail women and children are to be
permitted to go w ither they will :

> Denn niemand soll den Holofernes tadeln,
> Dass er nicht gross und edlen Herzens sei.

His shrewdness is denoted by the curt reply to the adulatory
speeches which he despises and yet loves :

> Ich wär ein guter König.—Was bleibt zu fragen ?

Bagoa suggests as a diversion the punishment of two old Jews, and Holofernes shews at once the malicious cruelty of the Oriental tyrant :

> Ich bin gespannt. Bagoa wird poetisch ;
> Das hat er ganz gewiss von mir gelernt.

At this moment, when his character shews itself in its most repellent aspect, Judith and Abra make their entry—an effective contrast. The Judith of this version has the power of bold and spacious conception ; she addresses Holofernes alone out of all the assembly, and assumes at once that he has a mind above such petty meanness :

> Warum, o Feldherr, schickst Du sie nicht fort,
> Die Dich so kränken ?   Betrübt es nicht Dein Herz ?

Holofernes is astounded, and arrested. Her pride attracts him when she states her reasons for seeking him out :

> Dein Glanz, Dein Ruhm, o Held,
> Und auch Dein Vorteil.   Ich bin Dir wohlgesinnt.

She makes her appeal, with her woman's shrewdness, to his pride ; the tale told by Achior of Holofernes' dishonouring women has angered her, and she has come to ask his protection for them :

> Da tatst Du gut daran, zu mir zu gehen :

The despot is accessible to this unusual type of flattery. A double-edged dialogue of great subtlety ensues. Judith tells him that he can conquer Bethulia in any event ; and to Holofernes' question of what she will do when her sack of provisions is empty (if she still refuses to eat his food) she replies :

> Dann wird sich finden, was ihn wieder füllt.

There is no mean deceit in the Judith of this drama. A shrewd wit, keen intellect, heroic faith, supply her with the means to beguile Holofernes. Significant, too, is the fact that she is big enough not to have shrouded her design in mystery ; Abra evidently knows her plan, for she asks in an undertone whether Judith still has courage to fulfil it.   The answer is characteristic :

> Ich wollt, es wär Dein Mut dem meinen gleich.
> So freudig ging ich nie zu Werk wie jetzt.

The cruelty of which she is a witness has its immediate effect in hardening her resolve.

Abra praises Judith's powers of dancing, and while the Assyrian generals discuss the news of Bethulia she has brought, Holofernes sits lost in thought. Then Judith dances, and he calls for wine ; she lures him into the tent. In the fifth scene, darkness has fallen ; Holofernes longs for wine, and is filled with restless desire. Stifling one access of misgiving (with the aid of Bagoa) he enters the tent for the night, and the act closes with a picture of him, suddenly struck with unwonted and unreasoning nervous terror.

Act IV is occupied with the difficult business of Judith's actual deed. Like most of the modern dramatists who have treated the story, Burchard sets to work to create an impression, and then indicates, indirectly, the course of the action. The choice seems indeed to lie between this method and pure narrative ; the earlier dramas, in which a compromise is attempted and half the action shewn, are almost always unsuccessful, at least to modern feeling Burchard, like Hebbel and Aldrich, creates the impression of horror largely through the agency of Abra. A memory of earlier dramas is evoked, however, by the choir of angels in the first scene, who sing, behind the stage, a prayer on Judith's behalf, while watchmen are before the tent of Holofernes. The second scene shews Abra outside the tent, watching for Judith's appearance. In lyric stanzas she expresses her anxiety ; she is interrupted by the soldiers, who envy Holofernes and advise her to go and rest. The first watchman says :

> Ich wollt, ich könnte Holofernes sein,
> Und dürfte drin au siner Stelle schlafen [1].

But his comrade answers :

> Nein, Kamerad. Du bist geehrt,
> Doch er ists nicht. Ihn hasst man nur.

The two characters are sharply differentiated. The first speaker expresses an ordinary, superficial judgment, envying material pleasures without further reflection ; his companion, on the other

---

1. The dramatic irony of this situation can be compared with that in Sturge Moore's drama (v. supra p. 118). The answer of the second soldier, however, gives the passage a deeper meaning.

hand, shews distinct originality of thought, and, when he later wonders whether Judith has any real love for Holofernes, an unusually philosophic mind. Finally both the soldiers fall asleep, and Abra waits, in growing excitement, while dawn appears in the distance. Her monologue is intensely dramatic ; from it we gather what are the possibilities involved in this deed of Judith's, and impatience, anxiety, terror, vivid imaginings, follow each other in rapid succession in her thoughts. A terrible vision of Judith killed by the sword is succeeded by a single cry from within the tent, and Abra, unable to bear the sudden terror that invades her, wakens the soldiers. They, however, refuse to believe her tale or to disturb the sleep of their lord. In the next scene Judith appears on the threshold, and they depart from the camp with their burden, ostensibly to pray. Judith only says :

> Der Herr war gnädig mir in dieser Nacht.

At break of day the watchmen outside the tent converse, in the opening scene of the fifth act—a dialogue full of dramatic irony.

> Weiss ich's ? Wir haben unsre Pflicht getan,
> Und haben diese Nacht das Zelt behütet !

is the consolation one offers to his fellow ; and when the guard is changed no report is made of anything unusual. Bagoa, in the third scene, takes it upon himself to leave Holofernes to his rest, and orders that he be not disturbed. He is sure of the Hebrew woman, because she has betrayed her country and therefore will not dare to return to it. But his order conflicts with those given by Holofernes himself, and a captain of the army demands admission on the approach of the enemy. Bagoa reluctantly goes in to wake Holofernes, and after Judith's return to Bethulia and the triumphant sally have been related, the curtain is raised, revealing the headless corpse of the Assyrian prince. Despair invades the beholders ; one voice—that of a messenger—is raised :

> Die Jüdin war's ! Sie hat ihn umgebracht !

The defeat and flight of the Assyrians follow. In the final scene, Achior leads the forces of Bethulia into Holofernes' tent ; Gothoniel and Osias pronounce his funeral oration and at the same time his condemnation, and mock the head raised high upon a pole. Abra glorifies Judith and her deed, but Judith refuses thanks and points to Jehovah as their saviour :

> ...Denn nicht hätt' ich
> Mein Volk erlöst, wär er nicht unser Freund !

On this, Achior again comes forward, and begs forgiveness for his doubts :

> Doch Du verzeih mir, Judith, dass ich fehlte ;
> Fahrt hin, ihr Zweifel ! Mein Königreich war Trug,
> Lug ist die Macht, vergänglich ist die Welt.
> Es hat nur Gottes Gnade ein Bestehen !

It is he who first kneels and praises the Lord, asking to be forgiven for straying from the way of truth and faith ; and the people of Bethulia echo his praise and prayer. Thus the Achior episode maintains its importance to the end, and the triumph of Judith over Holofernes signalises, in the mind of Achior, the triumph of faith over doubt. The character of Achior gains a significance greater than in other versions by this means, for he acts as mirror to the events of the drama, or as a chorus to interpret them. From being important in the narrative, he has become significant in the poetic interpretation of the story, for he emphasises its spiritual meaning. It is interesting to find a modern version which is mainly concerned with such a meaning—whose author does not hesitate to present an ethical conclusion. Perhaps here again we shall not be wrong if we regard such a development as proof of the adaptability of the theme to the needs of a particular age.

Two slighter treatments of the Judith story bring the tale of versions to the third decade of this century. The first, by Sebastian Wieser, published in 1918, is a five-act play with a decided streak of sentimentality, shewing also in its style and metre the influence of Wagner's music-dramas. The second is a version of the story by Rosmarie Menschick (1921), in which only female characters appear, and which is obviously compiled mainly as an acting version for feminine establishments. Neither of these plays possesses any great literary value ; but once more it is interesting to note the continued production of dramas on the well-known theme. Sebastian Wieser's is one of a series of biblical plays, and compiled with a view as definite as those of the dramas of the 16th century. Judith is the saviour of her people, but is drawn as a sentimental heroine withal ; Holofernes is a megalomaniac prince, whose speeches have a distinct flavour of the hysterical :

> Ein lästiges Geschlecht, die Götter,
> und erbärmlich ihre Priester !
> Doch ein Künstler war, der sie erfand ;
> ein grosser Geist, und ich beneid' ihn drum.
> Götter erfinden ! Wer das erdacht ?
> Doch—wären sie nicht,
> Holofernes erfände sie.   (I, 4)

The influence of Hebbel's Holofernes—or rather, the influence of the exaggerated characteristics in that figure—is plainly seen in the language and attitude of this grandiloquent tyrant :

> Verende ! Wicht !
> Stirb an der Pest !
> Fort !—
> ...Ich hätt' ihn durchbohren sollen.
> Aber es gibt nur einen Vagao !
> Er ist der einzige, der mir,
> dem Holofernes, die Wahrheit sagt.
> ......
> mein Wille ist—Wille der Welt !
> Mein Wort ist Sprache der Erde,
> ist Befehl—und wird Ereignis.   (I, 3)

The long tale of cruelties practised by Holofernes culminates in his slaying of Vagao in Act IV for a trifling fault ; the attempt to represent his intoxicated state at this moment is as unsuccessful as are the majority of such attempts.   He is, throughout, a figure of unreality, a stage tyrant masquerading, with Wagnerian staccato sentences, as a Titan.   Judith, similarly, does not make any strong appeal to our sympathies.   The author endeavours to pourtray a woman who does not use deceit in beguiling Holofernes.   She announces at once that she is his enemy (IV. 8), that she will only reveal her name when she belongs to him, and that she will only give herself to him when he has conquered Bethulia.   She stirs his jealousy by her tale of Achior's arrival in the city, and with a double meaning repeats her statement, made to the latter, that she knows no love—

> keine Liebe
> als die—zu Holofernes.

She then relates the history of Jael and Sisera, but stops short at

the crucial moment and omits Jael's deed from her narrative.
Thus without verbal lie she deceives him, lulls him with her song
and intoxicates him by her charms, which enhance the effect of the
wine he drinks.   Judith reminds herself constantly of Jael—whose
name occurs indeed like a refrain through the drama [1]—and in a
final hysterical outburst takes the sword and kills him on the stage.
The attempt to present the conflict in her is not altogether successful : her speech is broken, not from its very nature but artificially ;
and her language is that of a hysterical woman who would never
have been able to compass such a deed.   She is less grotesque than
her antagonist, but equally unreal.   The inability to give a convincing picture of her psychological conflict may perhaps have led
the dramatist to make use of a supernatural motif which recalls
the earlier religious dramas ; in the opening scene of the third
act—which takes place in Judith's apartment—the stage direction
is as follows : ' Judith kniet mit ausgestreckten Armen auf dem
Boden und betet.   Dann erhebt sie sich, geht ergriffen und schwan-
kend einige Schritte mit starren Blicken.   Eine überirdische
Macht hat sie gepackt... '.   This explicit direction is followed by a
long monologue expressing her doubts and interrupted by gestures
and visions ; the content of the succeeding scene is the passage of
an angel across the stage while darkness gradually descends.   In
the third scene, Judith reminds herself of Jael's example, and in the
fourth, the angel, to the accompaniment of music, bids her be as
Jael and slay Holofernes.   The dialogue is sung or chanted—this
is no doubt an attempt at emphasis, but the effect once more is
one of unreality.   A faint echo of Hebbel's heroine is heard in
Judith's subsequent monologue (III. 8) :

> Nun weiss ich, wozu ich reich bin,
> wozu ich jung—und eine Wittwe ;
> dass ich geschmückt
> niedersteige in einen Abgrund.

   But totally unlike the figure in the 19th century play is the
Judith who at the end replies to Achior's melodramatic confession
of his love for her by :

> Er stirbt !...
> Seine Liebe war sein Tod !

---

1. Cp. the Jesuit dramas and the Volksschauspiele, e. g. Judith (1650), (v. supra,
p. 61.) and Chronological Survey No. 53.

> Er starb für mich,
> so treu schlug ihm das Herz !
> Da du noch lebtest, gingst du
> an meinem Herzen vorbei.
> Nun bist du tot ... und stehst
> vor meinem Herzen.
> Dass du mich liebtest,
> war deine Schuld.
> Denn ich—bin des Ewigen.
> (winkt den Kriegern)
> Legt ihn in meine Gruft !
> An meines Gatten Seite
> soll er ruhen !
> (Feierlich)
> Jehova ! Du triumphierst !   (V. 11)

The part played by Achior differs somewhat from the normal, at least in its result. His love for Judith is, as has been seen, a familiar addition to the apocryphal narrative. As in Aldrich's *Judith of Bethulia*, he follows her into the camp of Holofernes, hoping to rescue her from its perils. Here, however, the resemblance ceases ; Achior, on finding Holofernes dead, acknowledges the deed to Ammon, his father, in a vague desire to save Judith (who has already escaped from the camp) ; and Ammon stabs him, wounding him to death. His final appearance is in Bethulia, in the last scene, where he dies at Judith's feet.

The most living parts of the drama are the scenes pourtraying the people of Bethulia under the stress of the siege. The vivid experience of war informs these dialogues with life ; naked greed and shameless profit-mongering characterise those among the populace who are not deadened by famine and misery. Distinct allusions to contemporary conditions are obvious in such speeches as that of Ismael (II.3) :

> Wer gibt ihm das Recht,
> uns zu bekriegen ?
> Gott nicht ! Menschen nicht !
> Jeder Fürst, der des Krieges Schwert
> hervorzieht aus der Scheide,
> soll durch dies selbe Schwert
> seinen Kopf verlieren.
> Dann hätten wir immer Frieden.
> Das Volk will keinen Krieg !

This scene appears to contain the key to the genesis of Wieser's drama, and demonstrates once again the living quality of the Judith story.

The second version by Rosmarie Menschick is totally different in aim and atmosphere. Since only female characters are shewn in action, much in the drama is of necessity narrated ; the interest is entirely centred in Judith herself, while Holofernes is a shadowy antagonist whose fate stirs no interest save in its effect on her. Judith feels a divine mission, and after much indecision resolves to seek Holofernes and ask mercy from him ; but instead of this she receives the sword of destruction from a Cherub, who accepts her offered sacrifice—her life—and bids her find and slay Holofernes. Sleep falls on him and all his camp at her arrival—Judith kills him, returns, and gives up her sword. But with it she also gives up her exaltation, and remorse invades her. She is tormented by the thought that she has murdered a man and is yet herself alive. Suddenly, a novel mode of expiation presents itself to her : Dalila, daughter of Ozias, in bitter jealousy of Judith and her beauty, has caused Salome, Judith's mother, to be poisoned. On her return, when she is overcome by repentance and self-accusation, Judith flees to Salome, and finds her dead. She recognises that this is the sacrifice demanded of her by God—not her own life, but that of the being who is dearest to her. Filled with this thought, she forgives Dalila, who after much agonising confesses her crime, and leads her back to life. The chorus sings a song of peace and love :

> Sühne und Opfer, in Liebe vereinet,
> Reichen sich schwesterlich hier die Hand ;
> Draussen die Feinde vernichtet, geschlagen.
> Friede zog ein in die Seelen, ins Land.
> Gross ist der Herr ! Gross ist der Herr !

The character of Judith in this version is saintly and self-effacing ; her deed is purely inspired by the divine command and is utterly at variance with her nature. Nevertheless religious obedience conquers, not only her natural horror but also her instinctive remorse, and she finds in Christian forgiveness solace for her grief. The play is one of a series of dramatised biblical stories [1], and has little intrinsic value ; but it is of interest to see the possibilities

---

[1]. The collection contains such plays as *David*, *Herodes* (a Christmas play with male characters only) and *Einer für Alle, Alle für Einen*, a ' Festspiel für Katholische Arbeitervereine '.

of such an elliptical treatment as is demanded by an exclusively feminine cast.

That a hundred and three versions of any one theme should have existed, and that many more than half of these versions should be extant and accessible, are facts which insistently demand an explanation. The foregoing survey, dealing primarily with the treatment of the story through the centuries, may have suggested some elucidation of the problem, in addition to those inherent characteristics of the tale which were noted at the outset as favouring its popularity. That the story was essentially dramatic was obvious from the apocryphal narrative : seventy-six out of the hundred and three records afford evidence of dramatic versions (including operas, oratorios, and periochae of plays), all later than 1530 ; and the early narrative versions themselves have a dramatic quality lacking in those of a later age, when drama is available as an alternative form to the poetic tale. But there are many well-known themes of dramatic quality which have been less widely treated ; the explanation does not entirely suffice, though it touches on a fundamental factor in the problem. Heroism is an enduring attraction in the story ; constantly the words ' herois ', ' fortis ', ' heldenmüthig ' occur even in the titles of dramas and poems. The spiritual value of this heroic quality is enhanced by the effective contrast of character and circumstance between the two chief figures ; and the contrast itself depends upon the antithesis of strength, sex, and religion. That such a tale should be used as an exhortation in time of need is not surprising. Accordingly we find the dramatists of the 16th century, with different motives from those of the epic poet of the 10th, equally delighting in a weak woman's prowess. That the spirit should be stronger than the body, that obedience to the divine will should prevail over human arrogance, that fortitude should prove greater than strength— these ideas, inherent in the story and dramatically vivid in the characters, explain much of its popularity in the 16th, 17th, and 18th centuries. On technical grounds, also, it commended itself to the writers of an age when drama was expanding into a highly complex form of art. With the ' problem drama ' of the 19th century the central idea is no longer that of faith rewarded by victory in an outwardly unequal contest : the conflict is one between opposing impulses in the central character ; while in our own day, we find the conflict—adapted to a dominant phase of modern

thought—becoming one of instincts.   On the other hand, perhaps by
a kind of reaction, the story is also treated in idyllic narrative and in
poetic drama, with a reversion (in the most recent treatments) to the
earlier habit of using it to point the moral of outward circumstance.

It is true that the majority of extant versions of the theme are
not of high literary value.   With one or two exceptions, the
greater artists have not treated it ; and often such merit as exists
is obscured, to modern eyes, by over-emphasis on secondary aspects.
But the interest, to the student of literary history, lies less in the
intrinsic value of the large number of versions than in the gradual
growth and changing significance of the subject.   The story seems
to express, as a great story should, something of vital interest to
every age.   Older poets saw the force, the triumph of Judith's
action.   They augured well for man from this tale of God's mercy,
shewn by the medium of a woman to the weakest of the nations.
The more thoughtful among the modern writers who have handled
the theme see its tragedy : the problem of a will greater than that
of the individual, compelling him against his instincts, bringing
confusion and irresolution to his mind—or, again, the problem of
the individual placed between two alternatives equally repugnant
to him, the dilemma of choice while he is himself uncertain of his
path.   They see the impotence of humanity, the inevitable conflict
in the more highly developed and more perceptive individual,
where the older writers saw primarily the vindication of God's
power and majesty, the possibility of miracle.   To say that there
has been a progressive disbelief in miracle is to touch on one aspect
of the transformation of the story.   That the explanation was
formerly so easy has also perhaps conduced to the preoccupation of
modern writers with the subject ; the minds lured to destructive
criticism have also been stimulated to creative effort [1].   Possibly
the greater artists have on the whole avoided the subject on
account of its long history ; but the increasing part played by
criticism in modern creative work is well exemplified by the versions
of the last century. Thus the Judith story in Germany and England
shews a long and gradual evolution.   To suggest the significance
of this evolution, as illustrating in some degree the growing complexity of the literary presentation of life, is the main object of this
brief survey.

---

1. That this is so with Hebbel can hardly be doubted (v. supra p. 96, note 4) ; it appears probable with Aldrich (v. p. 108, note 1).

APPENDIX A.

VICTRIX FIDUCIA BETHULIAE.

SIGREICHES VERTRAWEN AUFF
GOTT.

IN DER JÜDISCHEN STATT-BETHULIA / DURCH
WUNDERBARLICHE HÜLFF GOTTES VON DEM UNDERGANG ERRETTET.

VORGESTELT VON DEM CHURFÜRSTLICHEN GYMNASIO DER SOC. JESU
zu München.

DEN I. UND 5. SEPTEMBRIS.

ANNO M. DC. LXXIX.

GETRUCKT BEY LUCAS STRAUB / GEM : LOBL. LANDSCHAFFT
BUCHTRUCKERN.

ARGUMENTUM EX LIBRO JUDITH.

Quod opponere se ausa fuerit victricibus Assyriorū armis quibus
maxima quaeque regna & regiones se, subjecerant, Hebraea natio,
intelligit ex Achiore Ammonitarum Duce Holofernes, causam esse
magnam ejus populi in DEO suo fiduciam ; quam ille elusurus ea agit
pro Bethulia Judaea urbe expugnanda, quae ad decernandam in quin-
tum diem deditionem adegêre oppidanos.   Disturbavit verò consilium
Judith, auctoritate apud Cives & vitae sanctimoniâ conspicua, quam-
quam Juvenis vidua. Haec ubi sacro Sacerdotum Senatui fiduciae in
Deo collocandae constantiam persuasit, erexitque, exit in castra hostium, illic Holofernis amorem & gratiam sibi demerita, captata paulò
pòst occasione, sepultum temulentiâ & somno Ducem gladio ejus
proprio obtruncat. Redit cum truncati capite ad urbem, monet eruptione facta destitutum Duce exercitum opprimere. Parent Cives, fugant,
caedunt confusas copias, & cum grandibus spoliis victores redeunt,
relicto posteritati omni aeterno documento ; maximas spei vires esse
in rebus desperatis.

INNHALT AUSS DEM BUCH JUDITH.

Das einige Jüdische Volck dörffte sich setzen wider die grausame
Kriegsmacht / mit welcher fast alle Reich und Länder seinem König

Nabuchodonosor underwürffig gemacht der Assyrische Kriegs=Fürst Holofernes. Dessen Ursach als er von Achior der Ammoniten Fürsten verstanden / dieweil nemblich selbiges Volck grosses Vertrawen auff seinen GOtt hätte / von deme es nicht leicht verlassen worden / ergrimmet der grawsam Tyrañ so wol über den getrewen Ermahner / als über das gantze Jüdische Volck belägert Bethuliam sehr hart / entziehet das Wasser durch Abgrabung der Wasser=Teuchen / also dass Ozias der Hohe Priester das auffrührische Volck zustillen entschlossen ware den 5. Tag hernach die Statt dem Feind zu übergeben. Es hat aber disen Rathschlag hindertriben Judith wegen ihrer Klug= und Heyligkeit / bey der gantzen Statt sehr ansehliche / obwol noch junge Wittfraw. Dise von Gott angetriben / verweiset denen Hohen Priestern das allzugeringe Vertrawen auff Gott / macht ihnen Muth unnd Hoffnung / gehet darauff auss der Statt gegen dem Feind / wird vor Holofernes geführt / von ihme auff das freundlichist empfangen / und gehalten. Ersihet nach drey Tägen die Gelegenheit / unnd enthauptet mit eignem seinem Säbl / den in tieffer Trunckenheit entschlaffnen Tyrannen / gehet nach Bethulia mit dem Kopff / ermahnet die Burger einen kecken Aussfall zuthun in den Feind / so dann geschehen. Das ungeheuer Kriegsheer ist von dem kleinen Hauffen in die Flucht gejagt / unnd erlegt / beynebens ein ansehliche / und unzahlbare Beuthe nach Hauss gebracht worden. Welcher Sig dann ein Lehrreiches Beyspil ist der gantzen Welt / wie unfehlbare Macht und Würckung habe die feste Hoffnung / so auch in eusserster Betrangnuss auff GOtt gesetzt wird.

PROLUSIO.

Proponitur insolens Holofernis Ambitio inter Duces sui trophaea superbiens, quam in excidium Bethuliae acuentem acinacem fulminat, & depellit Tutor Hebraeae gentis S. Michaël, ereptum acinacem Holoferni intentat, atque ita Tragico-Comoediae propositum exponit.

In dem Vorspihl wird entworffen der Gotts-Lästerliche Hochmuth Holofernis ob dem Sigreichen Fortgang seiner Waffen stoltzierend / welchen aber der Beschirmer dess Jüdischen Volcks der H. Michael verjagt (mit eben dem Schwerdt ihme trohend / so er zur Verhergung Bethuliae geschärpffet hat) und hiemit das Vorhaben folgender Action fürbringt.

PARS I.

Bethulia Pressa.
Erster Thail.
Bethulia wird beängstiget.

SCENA I.

Oppugnaturus Bethuliam Holofernes docetur ab Achiore Ammonitarum Duce quanta sit populi Hebraei in Deo suo fiducia, quanta hujus potentia. Indignatur, & molestum monitorem in Bethuliensium manus abduci jubet, unà pòst cum ipsis interiturum. Simul, qui ab obsessis deditionem exposcat, ablegat.

Holofernes Vorhabens Bethuliam zu belägern / nimmet von Achior dem Ammoniter Fürsten Bericht ein / wie grosses Vertrawen das Jüdische Volck auff ihren Gott setze / wie mächtig auch selbiger seye. Ergrimet darob / und befilcht ihn in die Händ der Feinden weck zu führen / sändet zugleich seinen Legaten in die Statt / die Ubergab zu begehren.

SCENA II.

Intelligit decantata Judaeorum prodigia ex suis Holofernes, quae dum magicis artibus tribuuntur, suam etiam operam spondent Duci suo Magi Assyrii.

Bessere Erkandtnuss von den Juden Holoferni zu geben / werden die berühmte Wunder erzehlt / so Gott mit ihnen gewürckt / werden aber für eytle Zauber-Werck gehalten / wider welche auch die Assyrische Kriegs=Leuth ihre Schwartz-Künstler darstellen.

SCENA III.

Achior a militibus alligatus arbori, ab exploratoribus Bethuliensibus solvitur, & in urbem abducitur.

Achior wird von den Soldaten an einem Baum angebunden verlassen / aber von den Kundtschafftern auss Bethulia auffgelösst / und in die Statt geführt.

SCENA IV.

Obsessorum Bethuliensium angustiae & comploratio.

Deren Belägerten grosse Angst und Trauren.

SCENA V.

Augetur luctus adventu Legati, cum acerbis minis deditionem ab Ozia Sacerdote summo postulantis.

Das Leyd vermehret sich durch Ankunfft dess Kriegs=Gesandten / so mit grossen Trohen und Trutzen die Ubergab erzwingen will.

SCENA VI.

Sistitur Bethuliensibus Achior, refert Holofernis crudele propositum, unde major trepidatio obsessis.

Achior kombt in Bethulia an / bekräfftiget das grausame Vorhaben Holofernis wider Bethuliam / auss deme dann ein newe Bestürtzung erfolget.

Reduces ab effossis canalibus milites Assyrii, irritis resistentis Bethuliae conatibus insultant.

Die Assyrische Soldaten nach gefundnen und abgegrabnen Wasser= Teuchen / mainend den Handel gewunnen zu haben / verlachen den vergeblichen Widerstand Bethuliae.

CHORUS.

Exagitata timoribus Bethulia solicitatur ad desperationem. Aditum ad erigendam sibi faciunt Spes & Fiducia per sacros hortatores Moysen & Eliam, qui positis ante oculos antiquis, & recentioribus divinae opis prodigiis ad saniora trepidantem animârunt.

Bethulia wird durch manigfaltige Forchten geängstiget / zu der Verzweiflung angehalten. Kombt aber zur Hoffnung und Zuversicht durch kräfftige Ermahnung Moysis und Eliae / so ihr die mächtige Wunder= Hilff / welche das Jüdische Volck jederzeit erfahren / vorgestellt.

PARS II.

Bethulia erecta.
Anderer Thail.
Bethulia wird gestärcket.

Juditha hortatibus suis impetrat ab Ozia & seniorum consilio, revocari Decretum de traditione quinto pòst die facienda.

Judith verhebt den Hohen=Priestern das Misstrawen auff Göttliche Hilff / erhaltet durch erhebliches Zureden / dass sich die Statt eines bessern besunnen.

Animati Judithae fiduciâ seniores decernunt, obsidionem tolerare, datur Legato responsum.

Ozias sampt dem Rath durch Judith zu frischer Hoffnung ermundert / gibt dem Kriegs=Gesandten an Holofernes behertzte Antwort.

Repraesentatur Judithae in oratorio suo precatio. Unde animata surgit, ad demandatum sibi facinus sese promptam offerens.

Es wird entworffen das Gebett Judith / von welchen sie eyfrigist gemüthet auffstehet / und zu ihrer von Gott anbefohlnen Helden= That sich dienstwilligst erbietet.

SCENA IV.

Objicitur per somnium Holoferni Sisara Dux Chananaeus à Jahele interemptus, monens à fraudibus, & insidiis foemineis cavendum. Negligitur & ridetur somnium.

Holofernes wird gewarnet in dem Traum von Sisara einem Chananeischen Kriegs=Fürsten / sich von Betrug Weiblicher Nachstellung zu hüten / aber vergeblich.

SCENA V.

Refertur Holoferni Oziae responsum, excandescit, & extrema urbi & genti Hebraeae minatur.

Die Beantwortung Oziae wird Holoferni fürgetragen. Er ergrimmet grausamblich / betrohet den äussersten Undergang dem gantzen Juden=Geschlecht.

SCENA VI.

Egreditur Judith in castra hostilia, apprecantur fausta Cives & Sacerdotes.

Judith mit allgemeiner Glückwünschung der Inwohner verfügt sich auss der Statt zu dem Läger der Feinden.

SCENA VII.

Placatur interim ab obsessis DEUS poenitentiâ & precibus. Unde bene sperat Achior.

Die Belägerte halten underdessen bey Gott mit Buss und Gebett / umb glücklichen Aussgang an / warvon Achior gute Hoffnung schöpffet.

SCENA VIII.

Vulgatur in castris Assyriis Judithae adventus, malè hinc ominatur Mithras Popa Holofernis narrati de Sisara somnii memor.

Die Ankunfft Judithae wird ruchtbar bey den Assyriern / macht dem Götzen=Priester Holofernis gross Nachdencken.

SCENA IX.

Adducta ad Holofernem Judith, statum Bethuliae edocet, devincit sibi ejus animum & amorem : impetrat gratiam exeundi de nocte per castra in silvam proximam, ad fundendas ex ritu patrio preces.

Judith wird für Holofernem geführt / gewinnet alle Gnad und Huld / wie auch den Gewalt / durch das Kriegs=Läger bey Nacht in den nächsten Wald zu gehen / aldorten zu betten.

CHORUS.

Ostensa derisàque humanae potentiae imbelliâ, Spes & Fiducia munitissimum Bethuliae propugnaculum excitant, cujus inconcussam firmitatem gloriosi Hebraeae gentis, & SS. Heroës depraedicant.

Hoffnung und Zuversicht erweisen und verlachen die Eytelkeit Menschlicher Macht / erzeigen herentgegen die veste Burg / so Bethulia in Hoffnung auff Gott habe / so auch von den HH. und namhafften Kriegs=Helden dess Jüdischen Volcks geglaubet und gerühmet wird.

PARS III.

Bethulia victrix.
Dritter Thail.
Bethulia siget ob.

SCENA I.

Coena Holofernis, sub qua praeludit victoriae ovans ante pugnam juventa militaris.

Holofernes haltet das Abend Bancket / bey welchem als ein Tafel= Music die Glückwünschung dess verhofften Sigs erschallet.

SCENA II.

Bacchus & Cupido de temulento Holoferne triumphantes aditum morti faciunt, ad opprimendum tyrannum, quo ostenditur, sua illi vitia proprio exitio fuisse.

Bachus und Cupido triumphieren über den truncknen und entschlaffnen Holofernem / machen dem Todt einen Zugang / ihme den Rest zugeben / wollen hierdurch andeuten / wie er durch eygne seine Laster seye umbkom̄en.

SCENA III.

Usa occasione Judith, se ad inferendam Holoferni necem animat, obtruncat, & cum rescisso capite Bethuliam festinat.

Judith ersicht die Gelegenheit / ermundert sich zu kühner Helden= That / ergreifft den Säbel Holofernis / und hawt ihme in zweyen Straichen den Kopff ab. Eylet darmit nach der Statt.

SCENA IV.

Praefecti Vigiliarum ob temulentos ex convivio Duces solicitudo.

Der Wachtmeister ist wegen der bezechten Kriegs=Obristen in grosser Sorg.

SCENA V.

Vacillant Bethuliensium animi ob longiorem expectatae opis dilationem, Judithae absentiam, quos dum erigit Ozias, affertur de ejus reditu nuntium.

Die Burger in Bethulia begünnun widerumb zu wancken / und wegen Verweilen der erwarteten Hilff auff Judith ein Misstrawen zu setzen / da gähling die fröliche Botschafft von ihrer Ankunfft beygebracht wird.

SCENA VI.

Ingressa Bethuliam Judith, patratae rei seriem narrat, ostendit Holofernis caput ; jubet Cives eruptione facta destitutas Duce hostiles copias opprimere : fit excursio.

Judith kombt in die Statt / erzehlet den Verlauff ihrer That / weiset das Haupt Holofernis / ermahnet die Burger alsobald ein Aussfall zu thun / und das Hauptlose Kriegs=Heer dess Feinds zu überfallen / so dann geschicht.

SCENA VII.

Insultant excurrentibus Assyrii, fit mox turbatio. Urgetur Vagao ad excitandum è somno Holofernem, reperitur hic truncatus, ejus & totius exercitus consternatio, fuga.

Die Assyrier spotten erstlich der Aussfallenden / wird aber bald darauff ein ernstliche Forcht. Man setzt an die Kammer-Herrn / Holofernem auffzuwecken. Wird endtlich in dem Blut ohne Kopff gefunden / auff welches grosser Schrecken bey dem Kriegs=Heer erfolgt / dann auch die höchste Verwirrung und Flucht.

SCENA VIII.

Dum persequuntur fugitivos Assyrios Bethulienses, parat se ad excipiendos reduces victores juventus Hebraea, & capiti Holofernis insultat, cujus etiam contemplatio Achiori transeundi ad Hebraeorum sacra causa est.

In dem den Assyriern nachgesetzt wird / richt sich die Jugend zu Bethulia auff den frölichen Triumph / und verspotten den auffgesteckten Kopff Holofernis. Auss dessen Beschawung auch Achior in seinem Vorhaben der Juden Gott zu verehren bekräfftigt wird.

SCENA IX.

Redeunt ab hoste fuso fugatoque Bethulienses cum immensis spoliis, quae Judithae deferuntur, sed recusantur. Aguntur DEO grates & Liberatrici Heroidi applauditur.

Die obsigende Burger kommen von dem erlegten Feind mit ansehlichen Raub zuruck / selbiger wird sammentlich der Judith anerboten : wird aber von ihr nicht angenommen. Man preyset Gott umb erhaltnen Sig : wird beynebens mit grossem Frolocken der Judith danck gesagt.

CHORUS.

Ostenditur in opposita prologo epilogi antithesi triumphans de subjugata ambitione bellica Bethulia. Ad cujus spectanda trophaea evocantur Regna illa, quae Holofernis potestati se subjecêre, ejus potentiâ attonita, docentúrque majorem esse Spei & Fiduciae in DEO vim, quam potentiae omni, & viribus humanis.

Jenen Länderen und Königreichen / so sich nit getrawet Holoferni zu widersetzen / werden anjetzo von der obsigenden Hoffnung und Zuversicht die ruhmwürdige Sig=Zeichen Bethuliae dargezeigt / und bewisen / dass alle Menschliche Macht zu verachten habe / der sich auff Gott steuret.

SYLLABUS ACTORUM.

Assyrii.
Holofernes. D. Albertus Rorer, ad D. Michaëlis Musicus.
Achior. Franc. de Paula Benno Rott. Rh.

   Proceres Holofernis.
Vagao. Andreas Frölich. Cas.
Legatus. Casparus Rueff. Rhet.
   Silvester Doll.   Cas.
   Jud. Thad. Nidermair. Log.
   Josephus Kärpf.   Log.
   Bened. Donauer.   Rhet.
   Guilielmus Kerner.   Human.

   Decurio.
   Jo. Georg. Henr. à Jordan. Gram.

   Vexilliferi.
   Ant. Wilhelmus Plaz. Gram.
   Franc. Matthaeus Höger. Synt. Maj.

   Milites Holofernis.
Jo. Adamus Dietmair. ⎫
Joannes Walther.   ⎪
Matthias Corpi.   ⎬ Rhet.
Matthias Moll.   ⎪
Franc. Zwick.   ⎪
Ant. Mayr.   ⎭

Bethulienses.
Judith. Joannes Joachimus Inderstorffer.   Rhetor.
Abra. Fam. Joannes Andreas Faistenauer.   Rhetor.

   Senatus.
Ozias. Andreas Estner.   Rhet.
   Stephanus Fattor.   Cas.
   Georgius Staigenperger. Cas.
   Jo. Georg. Schreff.   Log.
   Franc. Dietrich.   Rhet.
   Franc. Mosmiller.   Rhet.

   Cives.
   Bened. Faber.   ⎫
   Bened. Pärtl.   ⎪
   Jo. Baptista Sartor.   ⎪
   Georg. Prösl.   ⎪
   Franc. Xav. Biderman. ⎬ Rhet.
   Josephus Rieger.   ⎪
   Maximil. de Campo.   ⎪
   Jacobus Mayr.   ⎪
   Joan. Georg. Thaimer. ⎪
   Matthias Pihler.   ⎭
   Georg. Philipp. Haimblinger. Hum

   Exploratores.
   Jo. Baptista Sartor.   Rhet.
   Josephus Rieger.   Rhet.

Ant. Widman.
Franc. Pauweber.
Balth. Fanger.
Franc. Karpf. } Hum.
Georg Homair.
Blasius Fischaber.
Sebast. Riedmair.
Melchior Kirmair. Synt. Maj.

Iuventus Assyriae.

Ferd. Eman. Aloys. Comes de Nagarola.
Raym. Franc. Xav. L. B. à Rehling.   Rud.
Ferd. Carol. L. B. à Berndorff.   Rud.
Franc. Guil. à Pelkhoven. Rud.

Magi.

Jos. Cajet. Gazin.   Poëta.
Joan. Aloys. Grueber.   Poëta.
Franc. Xav. Prungraber. Poëta.
Mart. Christ. Hueber.   Poëta.
Steph. Hen. Jo. Conradus Vrial. Synt. Maj.
Franciscus Nidermair.   Gram.
Georg. Sigismundus Neuburger. Gram.
Joannes Nidermair. Grammatista.

Salii Magi.

Matthias Mayr.
Joan. Schafhittl.
Domi. Zaun.
Simon Humps.
Joan. Georg. Miller.
Max. Harret.
Felix Viechter. } Grama.
Vitus Miller.
Michaël Perger.
Franc. Kauffman.
Adam Egolff.
Andreas Kaiser.
Andreas Kradt.
Franc. Xav. Gimpinger. Rud.
Ignat. Götschel.   Rud.
Jo. Georgius Paumaister. Rud.

Salii Epulares.

Joan. Casp. Castner.   Rhet.
Franc. Xav. Ig. Hiltprand. Poëta.

Iuventus Bethuliae.

Jo. Bapt. Petrus Pfister. Syn. min.
Egon Jos. Wilhelm. Syn. min.
Jo. Jos. Georg Walter.
Casp. Melch. Balth. Nepaur.
Anton. Remy. } Grama.
Emman. Felix Jos. à Geer.
Jo. Domin. Leidtl.
Max. Ema. Bonifacius Huefnagl.
Jo. Castner.
Franc. Philipp. Lindtmayr. } Rud.
Cajet. Sebast. Giggenbach.
Alb. Ernestus Jos. Im Hof à Ginzlhofen.
Franc. Franck.
Andreas Ostermayr. Principista.
Jos. Ant. Strassmayr.   Rhet.
Jos. Streidl.   Rhet.
Georg Michaël Mayr.   Hum.
Jo. Theod. Ant. Widenman. Hum.
Max. Emanuel Cajet. Pistorini. Syn. Maj.
Dominicus Carolus Widenman. Syn. Maj.
Franc. Igna. Fraunhofer. Syn. Min.
Franc. Guiliel. à Pelkhoven. Rud.
Zelus. Ferd. Joseph. Ant. Max. L. B. à Fraunhofen. Syn. Maj.
Humilitas. Franc. Matth. Höger. Syn. Maj.
Mors. Matthias Pihler. Rhet.
Cupido. Jos. Adamus Scharner. Rhet.
Bacchus. Matthias Corpi. Rhet.

Personae Musicae.

Musicam composuit & direxit. Georg. Schnevogl.   Cas.
S. Michaël. Josue. D. Georg. Dominic. Haindl, Music. ad D. Michaëlem.
Bethulia. Jo. Christoph. Pez. Syn. Maj.
Spes Divina. Jo. Petr. Permaneder. Syn. Maj.

Joan. Georg. Hagn.   Poëta.
Wenceslaus Warmundus Franc.
à Werndl.   Syn. aj.
Joan. Casp. Heiss.   Syn. Maj.
Paulus Ferd. Guil. à Gynzhaimb.
                          Gram.
Personae Scenicae.
Ambitio bellica. Fr. Guid. Ant.
Fugger, Comes à Kirchberg,
& Weissenhorn.   Syn. Maj.
Trophaearii seu comitatus Amb.
bellicae.
Fer. Jos. Ant. Max. L. B. à
Fraunhofen.   Syn. Maj.
Franc. Joan. Ferd. L. B. de Sir-
genstein.   Syn. Min.
Raym. Franc. Xav. L. B. à
Rehling.   Rud.
Carl. Octav. Ant. Im Hof à Ginzl-
hofen.   Gram.

Fiducia Divina. Sebast. Weinber-
ger.   Syn. Min.
Moyses. Samson. D. Andreas Friz,
ad D. Petrum Mus.
Elias, Sisara. Thomas Scheringer.
                          Log.
Samgar. Wolfgangus Mayr. Rhet.
Gedeon. Joann. Christoph. Than-
ner.   Hum.
David. Arabia. Timor. Joan. Jac.
Mauch.   Poëta.
Iahel. Media. Joan. Müller. Syn.
                          Maj.
Mesopotamia. Timor. Andr. Refl.
                     Syn. Min.
Syria. Timor. Leonard Seiringer.
                          Rud.
Armenia. Joseph. Benno Luz.
                     Syn. Maj.
Parthia. Augustinus Grien. Rud.

APPENDIX B.

JUDITH

TRAGOEDIA

Reverendissimo, Perillustri, Amplissimóque Viro, ac DominoDomino Gabrieli Hilgers, sacri, Canonici, ac Exempti Ordinis Praemonstratensis, Ecclesiae Steinfeldensis Abbati, Domino Temporali in Mahrmagen, Wehr, Wahlen, Urft & Wildenburg, Archi-Diacono Comitatuum in Schleiden, & Reifferscheid, Munificentissimo Musarum Mariae-Lauretanarum Maecenati, Patrono perquam Gratioso, dicata, acta ludis autumnalibus ab Ingenua, praenobili, lectissimáque Juventute Gymnadis Mariae-Lauretanae Fratrum Minorum S. Francisci Conventualium Monjaviae Diebus 26. & 27. Septembris 1763.

Aquisgrani, Typis J. W. Muller Urbis Typographi. [1]

INHALT.

Demnach Holofernes Oberster Feldherr der Assyrier beschlossen, die Stadt Bethuliam zu belagern, jagte er denen Juden einen grossen Schrecken ein ; aber auf Antrieb des Hohen Priesters Eliachim rüsten sie sich zum Widerstand. Holofernes dieses vernehmend erkündigt sich bey den Fürsten der Moabiter, und Ammoniter, wie es mit den Juden beschaffen seye. Als aber Achior der Ammoniter Oberst erzehlet, was grosse Wunder GOtt für die Juden gethan, lässt er ihn nacher Bethulia führen, damit er mit den Juden umkomme ; wird derowegen an einen Baum gebunden. Aber die Juden machten ihn loss, und wird wohl von ihnen gehalten. Indessen wolten die wegen der Belagerung hart getruckte Einwohner nach Zeit fünf Tägen sich dem Feind ergeben ; allein die fromme Judith bleibt unbewegt, bestraft, und muntert auf die forchtsame : begibt sich unterdessen nach dem Gezelt Holofernis, der aber zur Stund von ihrer Schönheit eingenommen wird. Da sie nun Gelegenheit gefunden, schlug sie ihm, von grosser Trunkenheit eingeschlafenen, das Haupt ab. Als nun das Kriegs-Volk der Assyrier vernommen, dass dem Holofernes das Haupt abgeschlagen, entfiel ihnen Muth und Rath ; dahero vor lauter Forcht und Zittern suchten sie ihr Heyl durch die Flucht, und eileten, den Hebräern zu entrinnen.

---

1. I am indebted for the transcription of this periocha to the great kindness of the Director of the Stadtbibliothek, Aachen (Dr M. Müller).

Judith, und das ganze Volk wegen des erhaltenen Siegs singen dem höchsten Erretter ein Lobgesang.

V. S. P. L. Judith.

ALLGEMEINES VORSPIEL.

Die Göttliche Vorsichtigkeit lehret, dass sie allein auf der Welt den Scepter führe, und über Alle Kriegsheer herrsche. Dass die Demüthigung vor Gott, und das wahre Vertrawen auf ihn endlich emporkomme. Dass übermässiger Hochmuth und Regiersucht nicht fern vom Stürzfall seye. Dieses bekräftiget sie mit dem Beyspiel des von dem David erschlagenen Goliath.

ARIA CANTO SOLO.

Wer nur auf Gottes Stärke bawet,
Und dem Himmel sich fest vertrawet,
  Wird von keiner Macht der Erden
  Jemahls überwunden werden.

Weichen muss Martis Wuth und Toben,
Wan nur allein auf den, der droben,
  In aller Demuth ist gericht
  Beständiglich dein Zuversicht.

TANZ DEN VERLAUF DES TRAUR-SPIELS VORSTELLEND.

ERSTER ABHANDLUNG.

1. Auftritt. Da die Bürger zu Bethulia vernahmen die Ankunft Holofernis, wurden sie mit Schröcken und Grauen eingenommen. Dannoch auf Antrieb des Hohen Priesters Eliachim rüsten sie sich zum Widerstand, und befleissen sich durch Fasten und Betten Gottes Hülf zu erwerben.

2. Holofernes, nachdem ihm der Juden Widerstand zu wissen gethan, erkündigt sich bei den Fürsten der Moabiter, und Ammoniter, wie es mit den Juden beschaffen seye.

3. Als aber Achior der Ammoniter Oberst erzehlet, was grosse Wunder Gott für die Juden gethan ; zürnen hierüber alle Kriegs-Oberste Holofernis, und trohen ihm den Todt.

4. Indessen die bey so trüb aussehenden Sachen höchst bekümmerte Bürger zu Bethulia bitten Gott inständig, um von dem bevorstehenden Unheyl errettet zu werden.

ARIA BASSO SOLO.

Harte Noth ! O bittere Zeit !
Ach grosser Gott Barmherzigkeit !
Lass deinen Zorn nicht länger brennen ;
Wir alle Schuld ja frey bekennen,

> Schau ! für Rew auch thuen vergiessen,
> Unsere Sünden abzubüssen,
> Ganze Ströhmen der Bitterkeit.
> Ach grosser Gott ! Barmherzigkeit !

5. Holofernes nicht weniger über die Wort des Achior ergrimmet, gibt Befehl ihn gegen Bethuliam zu führen, damit er mit den Juden umkomme.

6. Da nahmen den Achior des Holofernis Knecht, und bunden ihn bey Seiten des Bergs mit Händen und Füssen an einen Baum ; und nachdem sie ihn also mit Stricken gebunden hatten, verliessen sie ihn.

7. Aber die Juden kamen von Bethulia heraus zu ihm, machten ihn loss, führten ihn nacher Bethulia, und trösteten ihn.

ERSTE AUFFÜHRUNG DES LUSTSPIELS

ANDERER ABHANDLUNG.

1. Auftritt. Holofernes gibt Befehl, Bethuliam zu belagern, die Wasser-Röhren abzuschneiden, und an alle Brunnen Wächter zu legen, damit die Einwohner nicht vermögen, das nothwendige Wasser heraus zu schöpfen.

2. Welches die vom Durst hart geplagte Einwohner zwar beweget, sich dem Feind sammentlich zu übergeben ; dannoch auf Anmahn-en Oziae warten sie noch fünf Täg aus auf Barmherzigkeit von dem Herrn.

3. Da aber dieses der Judith hinterbracht, strafet selbige die forchtsame Oberste, dass sie Gott Zeit und Täg vorgeschrieben ; ermahn-et sie auf Gott zu hoffen, und um Hülf zu bitten : gibt auch zu verstehen, dass sie etwas gegen den Feind vorhabe.

4. Inzwischen kundschaftet Holofernes aus denen seinigen, wie weit es mit der Belagerung gekommen ; und da sie ihm die schleunige Uebergab vergewisserten, erfreuet er sich heftig über den baldigen Untergang der Juden.

TANZ.

5. Judith mit allem ihrem Geschmuck auf das herrlichste gezieret, gehet mit ihrer Magd zum Thor hinauss.

ARIA CANTO SOLO.

> Nur gehe hin, Gottes Dienerin !
> Judith nicht förchte, nur gehe hin.
> Dan Gott hat deine Weg gericht.
> Ein Aug, das dich wird sinken sehen,
> Wird eh' zum Todtes Schatten gehen.
> Der dir den schönen Glanz gegeben,
> Schenkt uns durch dich ein neues Leben ;
> Da dein Antlitz die Macht zerbricht.

6. Wird aber von den Kundschafteren der Assyrier aufgefangen, und zu Holoferne geführet : der zur Stund von ihrer Schönheit eingenohmen wird.

7. Und als sie von ihm gefragt wurde ihrer Furcht halber, betrüget sie ihn mit Verheissung eines glorreichen Siegs über die Stadt, und das Judische Land. Da nun diese Wort Holoferni gefielen, befahle er sie in seine Schatz-Kammer einzuführen.

ZWEITE AUFFÜHRUNG DES LUSTSPIELS.

DRITTER ABHANDLUNG

TANZ, IN WELCHEM DER UNVERHOFFTE TODT HOLOFERNIS
WIRD VORGESTELLET.

1. Auftritt.   Judith wird vom Holoferne zum Nachtsmahl beruffen. Sie erscheinet, isst, und trinkt vor ihm.

DUETTO 2.   CANTO.

Komm't ihr Musen, lieblich sollt singen,
Geigen, Lauten, lasset erklingen,
Wo Lieb, Lust, und Freud sich fügen,
Da vermehret das Vergnügen.
Auch du lauff ein, O edeler Wein,
Und mache die Herzen frölich seyn.

Esse, und trinke in guter Ruh,
Bis der Schlaf dir thut die Augen zu :
Was dich alsdan könte kränken,
Daran jetzt nicht thu gedenken.
Nur Fürst dich ergötze, trinke ein
Mit Lieb, Lust, und Freud den süssen Wein.

2. Und Holofernes war voller Freuden über sie, und überladete sich mit so vielem Wein, als er die Zeit seines Lebens nicht gethan. Als er nun von grosser Trunkenheit eingeschlafen, schlug sie ihm das Haupt ab.

RECIT.

Stolzer Hochmuth ! Was machst dich breit ?
Der Todt dir bringt ein baldiges End :
Nach Lust, und Freud erfolgt ist Leyd,
Also behend Gott das Blättlein wendt.

3. Die mittlerweile wegen ihr höchst bekümmerte Juden

4. Wurden itzo getröstet mit ihrer Ankunft. Sie zeigt ihnen das Haupt Holofernis, befahle selbiges auf die Stadt-Maur zu stecken, und den Feind mit Gewalt anzufallen.

5. Da henkten sie das Haupt auf die Mauren, und fielen mit einem g ossen Getümmel, und Heulen hinauss.

6. Als dieses die Kundschafter der Assyrier sahen, lieffen sie zum

Gezelt Holofernis ; und da man den todten Leichnam des Holofernis ohne Haupt in seinem Blut gewälzet funde, fiel eine
unerträgliche Forcht und Zittern über das ganze Kriegsheer,
verliessen alles, und eileten den Hebräern zu entrinnen : diese
aber verfolgten sie.

7. Judith, und das ganze Volk danken dem Herrn wegen des erhalten-
en Siegs, und singen ihm folgendes Lob-Gesang :

ARIA CANTO SOLO.

Jud.   O Adonai grosser Gott !
      Mächtig bistu Gott Sabaoth !
      Wer kan deine Macht gnugsam preisen ?
      Deiner Gütigkeit Dank erweisen ?
      Der du hast gestöhret den Krieg,
      Uns errettet, gebracht den Sieg.

      Assur kam her von Mitternacht,
      Seine Menge hast ausgelacht :
      Holofernem du hast erschlagen,
      Uns erlöset von Leyd und Plagen ;
      Darum werd dich, Herrscher oben
      Mit Herz, und Mund immer loben.

TUTTI.

Pop.   Also dir alle zum höchsten Dank,
      Erretter unserer Seelen !
      Singen wir ein neues Lob-Gesang,
      Kein Mund dein Lob soll verhehlen.
      Es lebt der Herr Gott Adonai,
      Der Holofernis Kraft, und Macht
      Durch Judith, die Tochter Merari,
      Hat erlegt, zu Schanden gemacht.

DRITTE AUFFÜHRUNG DES LUSTSPIELS.

BESCHLUSS.

Lehret, wie man in widrigen Zufällen, auch in den hartesten Nöthen
sich vor Gott demüthigen, seine Gnad mit vielen Thränen begehren,
und ein wahres, standhaftiges Vertrawen auf ihn setzen solle ; dan
der Herr diejenige nicht verlassen, die ihr Vertrawen auf ihn gesetzt
haben. L. J.

***

SYLLABUS ACTORUM.

Arnoldus Christian. Schmitz, Mon- Princeps Assyriorum. Providen-
javus.   tia. Choreutes. Spes.
Carolus Fridericus Strauven, Mon- Holofernes. Choreutes. Interlusor.
javus.

Christianus Andreas Wittichen, Monjavus.	Ozias. Interlusor.
Henricus Matthi, Monjavus.	Enuchus.
Henricus Küpper, Monjavus.	Miles.
Henricus Zimmer, Monjavus.	Miles.
Joannes Christianus Offerman, Monjavus.	Vagao. David. Musicus.
Joannes Chrysostomus Kussel, Monjavus.	Miles.
Joannes Gerhardus Matthi, Monjavus.	Bethulita. Musicus. Interlusor.
Joannes Godefridus Fischer, Monjavus.	Miles.
Joannes Martinus Stoltz, Monjavus.	Abra. Interlusor.
Joannes Michaël Geelen, Monjavus.	Achior. Musicus. Interlusor.
Joannes Nicolaus Schmitz, Monjavus.	Miles.
Joannes Zelen, ex Keldenich.	Centurio. Musicus. Interlusor.
Joannes Theodorus Dunckel, Monjavus.	Presbyter, Joliath. Interlusor.
Joannes Wilhelmus Josephus Bass, Monjavus.	Bethulita.
Joannes Wilhelmus Schmitz, Monjavus.	Judith. Musicus.
Mathias Heuck, Monjavus.	Miles.
Mathias Josephus Klinckenberg, Aquensis.	Centurio. Choreutes. Interlusor.
Mathias Josephus Scheffens, Monjavus.	Miles.
Mauritius Eiss, Monjavus.	Miles.
Michaël Ludovicus Kesseler, Monjavus.	Enuchus.
Nicolaus Bongart, ex Steckenbohrn.	Presbyter. Interlusor.
Nicolaus Bruch, Monjavus.	Bethulita. Interlusor.
Petrus Adamus Müller, Monjavus.	Cursor.
Petrus Wilhelm. Schmitz, Monjavus.	Dux Moabitarum. Superbia. Choreutes.

RELIQUOS SCENA DABIT.

INDEX

*

ERRATA.

---

p. 14	*l.* 28	*for* 47	*read* 46.
» 28	» 28	» peculiary	» peculiarly.
» 30	» 12	» that	» than.
» 32	» 13	» eipithets	» epithets.
» 35	» 9	» *poem*	» *poeme*.
» 70	*note* 2 *l.* 1	» ' cast down at	» cast down ' at.
» 88	*l.* 6	*om.* act.	
» 111	» 20	*sc.* [1]).	
» 123	» 5	*for* stage	*read* state.

TABLE OF CONTENTS.

Imp. par Desclée, De Brouwer et Cⁱᵉ, Lille. *(Fait en France).* — 4.007

47064

R|17
31|4|23